Making Jellied Preserves
from Garden and Hedgerow Fruit

Caroline Pakenham

SPRING HILL

Published by How To Books Ltd
Spring Hill House, Spring Hill Road
Begbroke, Oxford OX5 1RX
United Kingdom
Tel: (01865) 375794
Fax: (01865) 379162
info@howtobooks.co.uk
www.howtobooks.co.uk

First published 2011

How To Books greatly reduce the carbon footprint of their books
by sourcing their typesetting and printing in the UK.

Text © 2011 Caroline Pakenham

British Library Cataloguing in Publication Data
A catalogue record of this book is available from the British Library.

ISBN: 978 1 84528 475 6

Produced for How To Books by Deer Park Productions, Tavistock, Devon
Designed and typeset by Mousemat Design Ltd
Photographs on pages 15 (My collection of wooden spoons), 33, 67 and 105 by Marlisse Rawlins.
Printed and bound in Great Britain by Bell & Bain Ltd, Glasgow

NOTE: The material contained in this book is set out in good faith for general guidance and no liability can be
accepted for loss or expense incurred as a result of relying in particular circumstances on statements made in the
book. Laws and regulations are complex and liable to change, and readers should check the current position with
relevant authorities before making personal arrangements.

Contents

Cooking with your Jellies – Some Traditional Recipes 174

Introduction

There is joy in getting something for nothing, for creating something delicious out of very little, for not having to rely on a shop to be open in order to have to buy something which is high in artificial colouring and preservatives. There is also no need to spend money when fruits are prolific in the hedgerows and all you have to do is go out and pick them, a task that is a joy in itself.

Often, in late summer, especially in the afternoon sun, I can be seen walking the fields – sometimes with the dogs, sometimes with friends – picking wild berries with the scent of the grasses and the sounds of the wild birds and the occasional roe deer scrambling away from our path. This is just the best of times in the country. The fruit is trudged home and then the age-old autumn preserve-making begins.

Here is a wonderful description from an eighteenth-century household management book:

'Jellies may be described as solutions of gelatine in water, with wine, fruit and other additions, and their clear, brilliant transparency is one of their chief recommendations. However, jellies of this class do not comprise the whole list, for in addition there are the opaque nourishing milk and egg jellies and also those made from apples and other fruit.

'Calf's Foot Jelly, which is stiffened by the gelatine extracted from the feet by boiling, has the advantage of being perfectly pure. When nourishing jelly is required it is better made from good veal stock.'

So originally, the best setting agents for jellies originally came from calves' feet, but also from pigs' trotters. Vegetable setting agents were derived from seaweeds. While these setting agents are still used, we are concentrating on fruit jellies in this book and making them by using only the natural contents of the fruit without the help of additives.

The art of jelly-making is contriving to get a balance of pectin, sugar and acid in your fruits. Ripe and under-ripe can be mixed, as well as high-pectin and low-pectin fruits, as long as the balance is correct. You can easily mix and match to obtain flavour and colour, acid and pectin. You will soon enjoy experimenting!

I want to inspire you to create jellies quickly, cheaply and easily without any fuss and to capture the wonderful moments of the seasons in your pots of jellies. Large quantities of fruit can be organised into the freezer or the preserving pan. In the autumn I have wheelbarrows full of apples and pears and systematically turn them into delicious preserves for the fête, for my friends or for my larder.

In this book, I have collected together all my favourite recipes, following the fruiting plants round garden and hedgerow through the seasons. I have explained all the details of how this is done so that even real beginners can understand what to do, while experienced cooks will discover a wealth of new information and inspiration – and both will feel confident and proud of their end products.

Acknowledgements

Before I began this book my computer experience was practically zero; without the encouragement, support and endless patience of my family and friends, this book would not have been completed - I would have thrown away the computer!

Photography is not my strong point so I am extremely grateful to Marlisse Rawlins, a professional photographer and friends Zara Clark, June Fairgrieve and Hazel Januszewska for additional help in setting up and photography and Simon Saunders for his help with pictures on computers.

I would particularly like to thank my daughter Vics for giving up her week-ends to type most of the original text and of course my long suffering husband J, who found himself a reluctant jelly recipe expert and editor.

My thanks go also to Keith Goverd of KG Consultants who sourced useful historical information on processes of jelly making and the numerous friends and neighbours who listened and tasted and lent me their various tomes which were of such interest.

Finally, I would like to thank Nikki Read at my publishers How To Books who has been supportive throughout, despite my inexperience in book publishing and all my enthusiastic customers to Green Man, my business, who persuaded me to write down my recipes in a book.

A Brief History of Jelly Making

Preserving has been employed by many cultures throughout the world for thousands of years. *De Re Coquinaria*, or *The Art of* Cooking was written by Marcus Gavius Apicius, a famous epicure, in AD100. This earliest collection of recipes to survive includes recipes on preserves and jellies using fruits. Apicius described preservation for foods thus: 'Preserve your meats in mustard mixed with vinegar, salt and honey' adding that a particular favourite of the Romans was a honey sauce for cooked dormice!

The Greeks, in the first century, would fill crocks with pieces of fruit, especially their beloved quince, which were skinned and pipped and then covered with honey and sealed. They found that after about a year the contents turned into a 'wine honey' which they called *melomeli*. Both the Romans and the Greeks also used grape-must, or unfermented grape juice, which they boiled down to make sugar syrups for preserving fruit.

Honey was used by the native North Americans for storing fruit; whole wild fruits would be preserved in the golden liquid.

In the British Isles, of course, there was originally no sugar cane but there was honey and this was used for preserving all meats and fruits. The products were known to keep indefinitely, and also to be the best source of food energy.

Much later, when sugar arrived from the Middle East. it was very expensive and used only for the aristocracy. 'Your table' was a sign of wealth and the Royalty had their own confectioners as they appeared to have a very sweet tooth. Quince and medlar were fruits used commonly at the time.

In early times, people would have used clay pots as containers and covered them with paper dipped in a raw form of alcohol, then tied with twine. The alcohol provided a good protection against mould. Later, egg white brushed over the paper would have been used as an alternative to the alcohol. In the seventeenth century, animal bladders were boiled and stretched across the pots and tied firmly. The lip of the pots was also moulded by the potters not only to help pour but to stop mice from climbing up and into the pot.

It is thought that the art of preserving with sugar came to Britain with the Crusaders. Then when sugar refining began in earnest in places such as Cyprus and the Caribbean islands, sugar became very much more readily available to the masses. By the thirteenth century, most people were able to buy sugar in 'loaf' or 'pound' form. Preserving food through the winter had always been all-important, so once sugar was available, it became the preservative of choice, especially in the country areas where folk grew all their own produce. By the nineteenth century, when the price of sugar declined markedly, it became a peak time for jam and jelly making.

The West Indies became a very important supply of spices and fruits and this changed our preserving flavours, while all over the world, the peoples of different countries were finding their own preserving sugars. In Australia, the Aboriginal people used eucalyptus *gunnii*, the Persians favoured the sap of the sheep-thorn, maple sap was used in Canada, the sweet seeds of the raisin tree was used by the Japanese, a coconut tree in Chile and corn in the USA.

I'm only too glad that bladders have been superseded by screw tops and that the whole art of jelly making has been made so much easier. It must have been hard work and very messy in those early days!

Nowadays everything is much simpler and we take sugar and glass pots for granted. Sadly, however, we are both cooking and preserving less, too often buying highly processed foods – packed full of artificial chemical preservatives – for their look rather than searching out the freshest or most authentic ingredients and the real flavour of the fruits. Making your own jams and jellies can help to change this.

An advertisement from a Victorian cookbook.

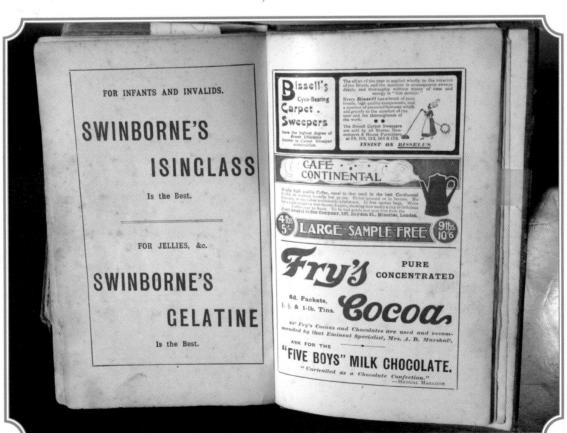

Is Fruit Foraging Legal?

The answer, of course, is 'yes', as long as you follow a few simple, common-sense rules. The Theft Act 1968 for England and Wales states:

> *'A person who picks mushrooms growing wild on any land, or who picks flowers, fruit or foliage from a plant growing wild on any land, does not (although not in possession of the land) steal what he picks, unless he does it for reward or for sale or other commercial purpose.'*

The Scottish Outdoor Access Code allows foraging but, again, not for commercial use.

Under the Wildlife and Countryside Act of 1981, it is an offence to uproot any wild plant without the land owner's permission, or to forage on a Site of Special Scientific Interest (SSSI). Some of these SSSIs are on National Trust land. Therefore hedges on a footpath or a road or lane are absolutely safe and within the law. On the other hand, straying on to a farmer's field, especially where there are grazing animals, is definitely not a good idea. If you are picking on an annual basis, you could always ask the permission of the owner of the land. Some councils and conservation bodies put up signs prohibiting foraging and you should respect such notices.

Remember, too, that over-picking in one place is not good as it damages the regeneration of the hedgerow. Always leave fruit for birds and animals so do not strip fruit completely or use shears to cut off whole branches.

I think using your common sense will guide you well.

Dennis – my amazing forager and chief taster!

Assembling your Equipment

Here is a list of the equipment you will need to start preserving, with some notes on the important details.

- A set of scales.
- Grater.
- Zester (optional).
- Large jelly/jam preserving pan, preferably stainless steel. Aluminium is not recommended as this reacts with vinegar and acid from the fruits.
- Large wooden spoon with a long handle.
- A cooker with a hob or an Aga.
- Stool or chair without a seat.
- Large piece of muslin or a jelly bag (see picture on page 23) for straining jelly.
- Four strong elastic bands.
- Several large plastic bowls.
- Saucer.
- Jam thermometer (optional).
- A skimming spoon, which is a large flat ladle with small holes.
- Plastic jug (600ml/1pt or 1.2/½pt).
- Funnel.
- Sterilising tablets (optional).
- Clean jars with lids.
- Wax circles/cellophane tops and elastic bands for sealing jars.

Pans

A stainless steel preserving pan is considered the best to use nowadays, wide enough to allow evaporation and deep enough to allow a rapid, rising boil, with a secure handle for lifting. Some people may have inherited their mother's aluminium pan, but we now know that under heat the aluminium metal can contaminate the contents so you should avoid this kind of pan. Copper looks beautiful but can spoil the colour of red fruits. Old enamel, zinc and iron are not good for maintaining flavour or colour.

Thermometers

When you make a jam or jelly, you need to boil it until it reaches the setting point, which is approximately 104°C/220°F. However, this does depend on the amount of pectin, the natural setting agent, in the fruit.

Essential utensils for jelly making.

My collection of wooden spoons.

Some people use a thermometer to test when the jelly is ready; I personally do not. I prefer the tried-and-tested saucer test, which is just as effective, as my recipes will explain. For this, you simply spoon a little of the liquid on to a cold saucer, and if it wrinkles when pressed, it is ready.

If you prefer to use a thermometer, put it in a jug of hot water whilst your jelly is boiling and when you believe setting point is near, put the thermometer carefully in the jelly mix without letting it touch the bottom of the pan. Return the thermometer to the hot water in the jug after use.

Straining

Once you have boiled your fruit, you need to strain off the juice. For very small quantities, I have used a large bowl and a metal sieve, with a piece of muslin to line the sieve so only the juice goes through into the bowl.

For bigger quantities, I attach a large piece of muslin, which can be bought at a fabric shop, to the legs of an upturned chair with four strong rubber bands (see page 23). If you don't have any muslin, like my neighbour when she first began making jellies, then you can use an ordinary pair of clean tights or a very thin tea towel. Place a large plastic bowl – on a sheet of newspaper in case of spillages – under the muslin to catch the liquid. Alternatively, you can buy a jelly bag but my method is very inexpensive and using muslin has the added advantage that it is much bigger than a jelly bag and therefore holds more fruit.

A Word about Jars

When I am selling my jellies, I buy hexagonal jars with lids in 350g/12oz and 225g/8oz sizes. The prettier the jar, the better the finished product looks. But please do re-use your jars and ask your friends to give you any nicely shaped jars with suitable lids that they would otherwise recycle. It is sometimes a bit fiddly soaking off the labels but if you leave them to soak in hot washing-up liquid then rub with a steel wool pad, you can have new jars for old!

Sterilising your Jars

It is important to sterilise your jars and lids before you use them otherwise your beautiful jellies are likely to go mouldy. Always warm the jars before filling them, too, even if you use ceramics, as the boiling liquid will burst the jar if it is cold. If you see condensation in the jar, this indicates that your jar is probably too cold, which will also encourage mould to form.

- Wash the jars and lids in warm, soapy water, then rinse in hot warm water.
- Arrange them on a tray in the oven at 140°C/275°F/gas 1, or in the simmering oven of an Aga, and leave to dry, sterilise and warm for at least half an hour. Many are the times that I have melted the lids so be careful to set the temperature as indicated!

If you wish, you can dissolve some sterilising tablets in water and soak the jars and lids according to the packet directions before you put them in the oven.

Having said that, I don't think a little mould on the top of jam and jellies is harmful. If it forms on the top, spoon it off and use the underneath as normal. When my children were young I would do this without them seeing otherwise there would be all sorts of howls of disgust. But in my experience, a little of the 'bad' builds up one's immune system with antibodies that nowadays seem to be discouraged, and maybe increases our lack of defence against common illnesses.

The 'All-in-one' Pan

I have to include this ingenious piece of equipment, which I have just found while researching this book; it is a beautifully simple concept from Finland. The Mehu-Liisa fruit steamer, distributed by Vigo in the UK, is made from stainless steel and very efficient and versatile. Juice is extracted from the fruits in the top basket by steam, it collects in the central reservoir and after the steaming has been completed, is decanted through a small pipe into a separate measuring bowl. The juice is then poured back into the base pan of the steamer after steaming has been completed. The jelly making then continues as normal with the addition of the sugar and the boiling of the juice until set. In other words, it is an all-in-one set of pans which replaces the separate jobs of boiling and straining. It is extremely clean, simple and effective.

I have been using a muslin and upturned chair to strain the juice for making jelly for so long that I believed I couldn't use anything else, but I have to say that I have been experimenting with the Mehu-Liisa fruit steamer and have found it very quick. It isn't too expensive and I would highly recommend it as a juicer and a steamer for all soft and stoned fruits in the making of jellies. Unfortunately it cannot be used for citrus fruits.

The Mehu-Liisa fruit steamer from Vigo.

The Mehu-Liisa fruit steamer in operation.

Choosing your Ingredients

Basically, you will be using fruit, sugar and water for your jellies – simple, natural and delicious, with no artificial additives.

The Properties of Pectin in Fruits

Pectin is the substance in the fruit that makes the jelly set. It is a clear, gluey substance found in the cell walls of the fruit which is released when boiled and softened at a simmering temperature. The pectin is like a long chain of units which, when released in the water under heat, need to amalgamate again to make a gel. They can't do this by themselves because pectin molecules give off a negative electrical charge, so they repel each other. To encourage amalgamation, the cook adds a good dose of sugar. Sugar molecules attract water molecules to themselves and, by boiling away water, the pectin chains gather together. Finally, the acidic fruit neutralises the electrical charge and allows the pectin to bond. Thus you have a set jelly which is closely allied to gum and has about the same food value as sugar.

Some fruits have a higher pectin level than others, which means jellies made with various fruits will set more or less easily. A rough guide is that the sharper or more under-ripe the fruit, the higher the level of pectin. Soft fruit is generally lower in pectin.

Fruits high in pectin	Fruits low in pectin
Apples	Apricots
Blackcurrants	Blackberries
Citrus fruits: grapefruits, kumquats, lemons,	Blueberries
limes, oranges, satsumas, tangerines and	Cherries
other orange varieties	Elderberries
Crab apples	Loganberries
Cranberries	Medlar
Damsons	Peaches
Gooseberries	Pears
Plums (especially wild plums)	Pineapples
Quince	Raspberries
Red currants	Rhubarb
Sloes	Rosehip
	Rowan
	Strawberries

It follows therefore that when you use a low-pectin fruit, you have to add either a high-pectin fruit or fruit juice or some citric acid in order to make the jelly set.

Some good fruit combinations might be strawberry and redcurrant or blackberry and apple.

The most popular form of citric acid to use with low-pectin fruits is lemons or lemon juice. If you have no lemons, you can use citric acid powder, allowing ½ teaspoon as an equivalent of 2 tablespoons of natural lemon juice to 3lb fruit.

Freezing High-pectin Fruit

There is a simple way I use to ensure that I always have plenty of high-pectin fruit to use with low-pectin fruit. If I have a glut of gooseberries and apples, I extract the juice and put it into the freezer in plastic containers until I need it. I can then defrost as needed and add to the low-pectin juice.

Most fruits are easily frozen whole if you are unable to make your preserves with them straight away. Seville oranges are a good example. They are very high in pectin and freeze easily. When they are in season, in December, January and February (although sadly not in our hedgerows!), I buy a crate from the local market, put them into plastic bags and freeze them so that they can be used through the year at my convenience. They can either be turned into marmalade or just juice for flavouring other jellies. They are simple to defrost as they separate easily.

Sugar

Sugar is used for preserving the fruit as well as sweetening. I cut down on the amount of sugar I use because many jellies are too sweet and that overpowers the flavour of the fruit. It is said that if you put more sugar into a preserve, you will gain a better set but in fact it will only make it sweeter. The correct amount of sugar for preservation purposes is 65 per cent.

Always use granulated sugar or loaf sugar. I have used brown sugar on occasion but it is much more treacly. There is absolutely no need to buy the preserving sugar, containing added pectin, which is frequently sold for making marmalade; not only is it sweeter but it is nearly twice the price of granulated sugar. You do not need the extra pectin in the sugar if it is already in the fruit. You'll find all the information you need in the recipes on coping with low-pectin fruits.

TIP: If you use US cups, 225g/8oz sugar = 1 cup.

Water

I have generally used 300–600ml/1/2–1pt of water to every 3lb/1.5kg of fruit in my recipes but this only has to be a rough estimate. Generally speaking, you simply add the fruit to the pan, then cover it with water so, rather than giving a quantity, my recipes normally say 'water sufficient to cover the fruit'. You can measure the water if you wish, but if you have added too much water it will just take a little longer to boil away.

Soft fruits or ripe fruit, with less pectin, need less water, while strawberries and raspberries need none at all unless cooked with other fruits. Hard fruits need to be covered with more water and cooked for longer in order to tenderise them.

TIP: If you use US cups, 250m/8fl oz = 1 cup.

The Pectin Test

If you don't know if the fruit you are using has pectin in it then this simple test will tell you.
- Cook the fruit until tender.
- Take a tablespoon of the juice and put it in a cup or on a saucer.
- Add 3 teaspoons of methylated spirit or grain alcohol to the juice and watch the reaction.
- If the mixture coagulates into a transparent blob, then you have good pectin.
- If there are just two or three little blobs, then the pectin is low.
- If there are just little flecks, then your pectin is insufficient.

Fruits with high pectin, such as cooking apples, can yield extra juice. Once you have cooked your fruit and extracted the juice, return the pulp to the pan with more water and boil for a second time to provide even more juice for jelly making.

Boiling mixed fruits in a preserving pan.

How to Make Jelly

Now, the fun begins! First find and recognise your fruit!

The hedgerows are alive with fruit, especially in the autumn, so get out into the countryside and see what you can find. Always carry a bag in your pocket when you are out walking as you never know when you are going to find something delicious just ready to harvest. Try to pick the slightly under-ripe fruit because it holds more pectin, and avoid picking over-ripe fruit as it will go off very quickly. You don't always want masses of fruit to make a good jelly so just enjoy the gathering and see what you can make with your findings. You can always add something from your fruit bowl, such as an extra orange or apple.

I am also very lucky in being able to go to an excellent fruit and vegetable market just down the road from me every week, where I can buy boxes of fruit at extremely good prices to add to the fruit I have gathered!

There are often insects in wild fruit and flowers so make sure that you leave them to crawl away after picking. Although it can't happen with jelly making because you sieve all the fruit, I did find half a wasp in my boiling strawberry jam one day! It gives you that weird and worrying feeling, like finding half a caterpillar in your salad!

The Basic Jelly Recipe

Here are the basic principles on which all jelly recipes are based. Once you understand the process, you can use any of my recipes or start experimenting with your own.

Quantities

As a general indication, 2kg/4½lb of fruit with 1kg/2¼lb of sugar will make 1.5kg/3lb of jelly, although this will vary according to the fruit type. My recipes follow this approximate ratio. With all the recipes in this book, feel free to use smaller quantities but retain the same proportions.

Preparing your Ingredients

- The main basic ingredients you require for jelly making are fruit, granulated sugar and water. Collect your chosen fruits, making sure you allow for low-pectin fruits by having some high-pectin fruit or lemon juice.
- Wash the fruit and pick out any bruised or bad pieces. Make sure there are no insects left lurking! If you use bad fruits, your jelly will not last, although the odd twig and leaf is fine!
- Put the fruit into a large preserving pan. There is no need to weigh the fruit but only fill the pan up to a maximum of two-thirds full.

- Cover the fruit with cold water. If you are using soft fruit, such as raspberries, you will need slightly less water but I have specified the quantities in the relevant recipes.

Softening the Fruit

- Bring the fruit and water to the boil, then turn down the heat and allow to simmer, preferably with a lid on, for about 10–60 minutes, depending on the fruit, until it is just tender with some fruits, soft and mushy with others, as the recipes will indicate.
- Remove from the heat and leave to cool.
- Mash the fruit with a potato masher to squeeze out all the juice.

CAUTION: You must use your common sense and be very careful when jelly making as you can easily scald yourself when handling and pouring a large amount of boiling liquid. Remember, too, that the steam is just as potentially dangerous as the hot water. Once the jelly and sugar have started to boil, they are ferociously hot; on no account should you touch jam or jelly while it is cooking.

Cooked apple at the cooling stage.

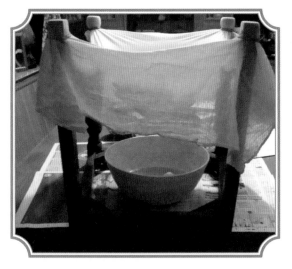

Straining jelly through muslin fixed
to an upturned stool.

Using a sieve and a bowl
to strain very small quantities.

Straining

- Set up your muslin or jelly bag over an upturned stool with a large bowl underneath. Make sure it is placed where it will not be knocked over or interfered with. Don't let the dog lie underneath as I did once! A Newfoundland dog and jelly dripping do not go well together. You can imagine what a mess there was when he got up and tipped the chair off the table!
- Pour the mashed fruit into the muslin or jelly bag and leave it to drip through into the bowl. Leave to drip for several hours or preferably overnight. Do not squeeze the bag or your jelly will be cloudy.

Sterilising the Jars

- As outlined before, wash your jars and lids, then sterilise and warm them on a rack in the oven at 140°C/275°F/gas 1, or in the simmering oven of an Aga, for approximately half an hour.

Removing the Pulp

- Take away the muslin but, as I said, do NOT be tempted to squeeze the juice out of the muslin as this will make your jelly cloudy. Of course, if you are not fussy and are not 'exhibiting' the jelly in a local show, then there is no harm in squeezing to get more flavour.
- You can then discard the pulp.

Preparing to Boil

- At this point, if you need to add the juice of a lemon, for extra pectin, add it to the strained juice through a sieve.
- Pour the juice into a measuring jug to establish the quantity, then transfer it to the cleaned preserving pan and put on to a low heat while you measure the granulated sugar.

- For most recipes, add 350g/12oz of granulated sugar for every 600ml/1pt of juice. Keep it on a low heat and stir constantly until the sugar has dissolved and it no longer feels gritty on the bottom of the pan. This is very important because if the sugar has not dissolved when you turn up the heat, it will burn on the bottom and spoil the flavour of the finished product. Yes, I have done that!

Boiling the Jelly

- Once the sugar has dissolved, turn up the heat and bring to a rapid boil – that means the liquid should be bubbling vigorously. Keep an eye on it and make sure it does not come so high up the pan that it is likely to spill over the top.
- Continue to boil until the jelly reaches setting point. This should take an average of 10 minutes but depends on the volume of liquid.

Setting Point

- You can recognise setting point when the bubbles start to cling together and the liquid rises. It is important to watch carefully at this time, so you can take the pan off the heat or turn the heat down as necessary.
- When you start cooking, pop a saucer in the fridge. Then, when you think your jelly is beginning to set, take a tablespoonful of the jelly, put it on the cold saucer and either place it outside on a flat surface (not in the rain!) or back in the fridge and leave for a couple of minutes to cool. If the jelly wrinkles when the saucer is tilted or you push it with your finger, then it is ready, so take the jelly off the heat straight away.

Bubbles gathering to reach setting point.

Using the finger test to check whether a jelly is setting.

- If it doesn't wrinkle, then continue to boil for another 5 minutes, then test again. Take your time and never hurry this stage because all fruits are going to be different.
- Another way to test for setting point is by dipping a wooden spoon into the mixture and letting the liquid drop from about chin level. If the cooking jelly clings to the spoon and then drops in a 'flake', then the jelly is ready.

TIP: If your jelly has been cooking for ages and doesn't look as if it is going to set, add the juice of a lemon through a sieve and continue to boil. However, this will only help with a low-pectin fruit.

Skimming

- Take the pan off the heat and remove the scum from the surface – known as skimming or scumming – with a skimming spoon by drawing the spoon gently over the surface of the liquid to remove the scum. Wild fruits are usually the worst culprits for scum.

De-scumming boiled jelly.

Adding Other Ingredients

- If you are adding chopped herbs or other chopped ingredients to your jelly, you would do so now. Stir the jelly until it begins to cool, keeping it moving so it does not form a skin. Add the chopped ingredients and stir until they are evenly distributed and begin to sink through the jelly.
- If you are adding alcohol, you can do so after skimming or before.

Filling and Labelling the Jars

- Put the preserving pan on to a safe, flat surface and immediately start to fill the sterilised, warmed jars. I find it easiest to use a plastic jug with a lip to scoop up the hot jelly and pour it into the jars, as this avoids too many drips and spillages. Make sure you fill the jars to the very top because a good seal is important for preservation. Jelly, similar to jam, shrinks when it is cool.
- Immediately put on the lids. You can use a waxed paper jam disc on the top of each jar before closing the lid if you wish but they are not really necessary.
- Leave until cool, then tighten the lids again firmly. This is very important as bacteria or air could get in if you don't ensure a firm seal as soon as possible after cooling.
- When cold, label with the name of the jam and the date – don't assume you'll remember in a few months' time.

Storing your Jelly

- Store in a larder or store cupboard which is cool, dry and dark.
- Most jellies will last for up to a year or even more. Don't forget it's a preserve and it will last unopened without putting in the fridge. I found one at the back of my larder once and it was five years old! Oh well, no one's perfect!
- Once opened, your jelly does need to be kept in the cool with the lid firmly in place or it will dry out.

Use a plastic jug to pour the hot jelly into the jars

If Things Go Wrong

Generally, making jelly is a straightforward process but of course things can go wrong so here's a guide to help you salvage the situation if you have a problem. Sometimes you will be able to correct the mistake, otherwise you may simply have to learn the lesson for the next time.

Crystallisation

Crystals arrive on the top of the jelly.
- The sugar did not dissolve properly when making the jelly.
- There was too much sugar in proportion to fruit.
- The jelly has been stored in a temperature that is too warm.
- The jelly is too old.

Fermentation

The jelly has a slightly off fizzy taste.
- The fruit was over-ripe.
- Not enough sugar has been added.
- The jars were not sterilised.
- The covers have not sealed properly.

Mould

There is mould on the surface of the jelly.
- The fruit was too ripe when cooked.
- The covers were not put on quickly enough after cooling or the lids have not been sterilised properly.
- The storage conditions are too damp; jellies must be kept where it is dry and dark.

Colour

The jelly is cloudy.
- The muslin was probably not thick enough and allowed too much of the fruit through.
- The muslin might have been squeezed to get more juice through.
- The jelly has been stored in too bright a light.

The Jelly Will Not Set

The jelly will not reach setting point.
- There is too much low-pectin fruit and too little acid.
- The fruit is too ripe, which means a low acid content.

In either of these cases, you can add a little lemon juice through a sieve.
- Prolonged cooking has damaged the pectin.

Unfortunately when this happens there is only one solution: the compost heap.

SPRING JELLY RECIPES

This chapter contains a range of recipes using the produce that comes into season in the spring. Get out to the hedgerows early to bag the best for your jellies before the birds!

Lemon and Earl Grey jelly ready for tea.

Sweet Earl Grey and Lemon

This is such a delicious combination of flavours and highly recommended for when grandma comes for tea. Serve it on hot scones – freshly made, of course!

2kg /4½lb cooking apples

4 large tablespoons Earl Grey leaf tea

2 lemons

Water

Sugar

---

1. Put the apples into a preserving pan, cover with water and bring to the boil. Simmer until tender, about 45 minutes.

2. Add the leaf tea, stir, then remove from the heat and leave to cool and infuse.

3. Strain through a muslin for 12 hours or overnight.

4. Put the jars and lids in the oven to sterilise.

5. Measure the juice and return it to the clean preserving pan. Add 350g/12oz of sugar and the juice of 1 lemon to every 600ml/1pt of juice.

6. Place over a low heat and stir continuously until the sugar has completely dissolved and there is no grittiness.

7. When the sugar has fully dissolved, bring to the boil and boil rapidly until setting point, about 10 minutes.

8. Slice the other lemon, place in a small pan with a little water. Bring to the boil, then boil for about 3 minutes. This is sterilising the fruit you will add to the jars later on.

9. Test the jelly on a cold saucer for crinkling and, when ready, remove from the heat. If it is not ready, then leave it to boil for another 5 minutes and test again.

10. Add one slice of cooked lemon into each warmed jar.

11. Skim the jelly, then pour immediately into the jars, filling to the top. Put on the lids and leave to cool before labelling.

Honey and Apple

Did you know that a bee flies 80,500km/50,000 miles and visits two million flowers for every 450g/1lb of honey? No wonder we coined the expression 'busy bee'! Personally I have always loved honey with its beautiful natural colours and the variety of flavours that change depending on the flowers that the bees pollinate. This is just one of the fun characteristics of honey, but I also like it because it is natural and healthy. I have a friend who keeps bees, so we exchange my jellies for her honey. (A spoonful of local honey every day can cure you of the miseries of hay fever, too.) This combination of apple and honey is perfectly simple. Brush it lavishly over an apple tart for the perfect dessert.

900g/2lb cooking apples
Juice of 1 lemon
225g/8oz clear honey
Water

---

1. Put the apples into a preserving pan, cover with water and bring to the boil. Simmer until tender, about 20 minutes.

2. Remove from the heat, mash with a potato masher, then leave to cool.

3. Strain through a muslin for 12 hours or overnight.

4. Put the jars and lids in the oven to sterilise.

5. Measure the juice, return it to the clean preserving pan, then add the lemon juice through a sieve.

6. Place over a low heat and add the honey, stirring continuously until dissolved.

7. When the honey has fully dissolved, bring to the boil and boil rapidly until setting point, about 10 minutes.

8. Test the jelly on a cold saucer for crinkling and, when ready, remove from the heat. If it is not ready, then leave it to boil for another 5 minutes and test again.

9. Skim the jelly, then pour immediately into the warm jars, filling to the top. Put on the lids and leave to cool before labelling.

Rhubarb and Ginger

The angelica or sweet cicely in this recipe cut the acid in the fruit, allowing you to reduce the amount of sugar used. However, if you do not happen to have any of these plants growing in or near your garden, just use the normal recommended amount of sugar. This is extremely tasty in a rhubarb sponge with added crystallised ginger for richness and flavour. The tangerine just brings out the rhubarb tang.

900g/2lb rhubarb
4 sweet apples
6 slices of fresh ginger
1 branch of angelica or sweet cicely (optional)
2 tangerines or 1 orange (optional)
5–6 pieces of crystallised ginger
Water
Sugar

1. Slice the rhubarb and put in the preserving pan with the apples, ginger, the branch of angelica or sweet cicely and the tangerines or orange, if using. Cover with water and bring to the boil. Simmer until tender, about 40 minutes.

2. Mash with a potato masher, then leave to cool.

3. Strain through a muslin for 12 hours or overnight.

4. Put the jars and lids in the oven to sterilise.

5. Measure the juice and return it to the clean preserving pan. Add 350g/12oz of sugar to every 600ml/1pt of juice.

6. Place over a low heat and stir continuously until the sugar has completely dissolved and there is no grittiness.

7. When the sugar has fully dissolved, bring to the boil and boil rapidly until setting point, about 10 minutes.

8. Test the jelly on a cold saucer for crinkling and, when ready, remove from the heat. If it is not ready, then leave it to boil for another 5 minutes and test again.

9. Skim the jelly. Slice the crystallised ginger and add to the warmed jars, then pour the setting jelly over the ginger, filling to the top. Put on the lids and leave to cool before labelling.

Rhubarb and branches of sweet cicely ready for cooking.

Orange Shred and Apple

Many old recipes combine the wonderful flavours of orange and apple in pies and pastries as they work so well together. Plus you can also add some spices to the boiling fruits if you feel like something slightly different. Cloves are a good spice to try in this recipe.

3 oranges
1.5kg/3lb sweet or cooking apples
Water
Sugar

1. Pare off the rind of the oranges, cut into julienne strips – long, thin shreds – and reserve.

2. Put the apples and oranges into a preserving pan, cover with water and bring to the boil. Simmer until tender, about 30 minutes.

3. Mash with a potato masher, then leave to cool.

4. Strain through a muslin for 12 hours or overnight.

Preparing julienne strips of orange rind.

5. Put the jars and lids in the oven to sterilise.

6. Measure the juice and return it to the clean preserving pan. Add 350g/12oz of sugar to every 600ml/1pt of juice.

7. Place over a low heat and stir continuously until the sugar has completely dissolved and there is no grittiness.

8. Add the julienne strips of orange rind.

9. When the sugar has fully dissolved, bring to the boil and boil rapidly until setting point, about 10 minutes.

10. Test the jelly on a cold saucer for crinkling and, when ready, remove from the heat. If it is not ready, then leave it to boil for another 5 minutes and test again.

11. Skim the jelly, then stir to cool slightly and to distribute the fruit strips through the jelly.

12. Pour immediately into the warm jars, filling to the top. Put on the lids and leave to cool before labelling.

Salad Burnet

Salad burnet (Poterium sanguisorba) is a herb that has a delicate flavour like crisp cucumber. There is a greater burnet and a lesser burnet, both of which can be found growing wild in the fields or ditches. The plant tends to grow very 'leggy' and has lots of branches but these are still very tasty and should be taken off to allow the leaves to come again. So this recipe is a perfect way of using those cuttings. Salad burnet is very tasty when used in a salad with lettuce or made into a jelly to be served with cold meats. When making jellies, it is quite fun to capture unusual flavours like this so you can preserve them through the winter months to enjoy when you cannot find the plants growing outside.

900g/2lb cooking apples
2 large, soft stems and leaves of salad burnet, about 30cm/12in long
2 handfuls of salad burnet
Water
Sugar

---

1. Put the apples and salad burnet stems into a preserving pan, cover with water and bring to the boil. Simmer until tender, about 20 minutes.

2. Mash with a potato masher, then leave to cool and infuse.

3. Strain through a muslin for 12 hours or overnight.

4. Put the jars and lids in the oven to sterilise.

5. Measure the juice and return it to the clean preserving pan. Add 350g/12oz of sugar to every 600ml/1pt of juice.

6. Place over a low heat and stir continuously until the sugar has completely dissolved and there is no grittiness.

7. When the sugar has fully dissolved, bring to the boil and boil rapidly until setting point, about 10 minutes.

8. Test the jelly on a cold saucer for crinkling and, when ready, remove from the heat. If it is not ready, then leave it to boil for another 5 minutes and test again.

9. Skim the jelly.

10. Finely chop the salad burnet.

11. Stir the jelly until nearly cool and beginning to set, then add the chopped salad burnet and stir again to distribute the herb.

12. Pour immediately into the warm jars, filling to the top. Put on the lids and leave to cool before labelling.

Salad burnet growing in my garden.

Fig

To me, figs are reminiscent of hot sunny days in the Mediterranean. They have a uniquely sweet taste and are full of edible seeds, so making them into a jelly allows you to retain the wonderful flavour without the crunch of the seeds. They also contain calcium and are a good source of vitamins A, B and C, but remember they are also a good laxative! If you are lucky enough to have figs growing in the garden, choose the slightly under-ripe ones for preference. Figs do not contain much pectin, hence the inclusion of lemons to encourage the jelly to set.

900g/2lb fresh figs

4 lemons

Water

Sugar

---

1. Grate the lemon rind and reserve.

2. Put the figs into a preserving pan with the whole lemons, cover with water and bring to the boil. Simmer until tender, about 10 minutes.

3. Mash with a potato masher, then leave to cool and infuse.

4. Strain through a muslin for 12 hours or overnight.

5. Put the jars and the lids in the oven to sterilise.

6. Measure the juice and return to the clean preserving pan. Add 350g/12oz of sugar to 600 ml/1pt of juice.

7. Place over a low heat and stir continuously until the sugar has completely dissolved and there is no grittiness.

8. Add the reserved lemon rind.

9. When the sugar has fully dissolved, bring to the boil and boil rapidly until setting point, about 10 minutes.

10. Test the jelly on a cold saucer for crinkling and, when ready, remove from the heat. If it is not ready, then leave it to boil for another 5 minutes and test again.

11. Skim the jelly, then pour immediately into the warm jars, filling to the top. Put on the lids and leave to cool before labelling.

Bitter Lime with Pernod

I buy limes by the boxful as they are so versatile. Once I have made jelly, the rest go into marmalade. My son, who lives in Australia, has them growing in the garden in profusion. He now makes marmalade, which is amazing for a 'non cook'! Limes do not keep as long as lemons so always buy the solid green ones and store them in the fridge to keep them fresh.

I always associate Pernod and that gentle aniseed flavour with small Parisian pavement cafés and long summer lunches! Mixed with cool, exotic, fresh limes, you have a perfect jelly to use with grilled fish or dipping prawns.

900g/2lb fresh limes, about 16

120ml/4fl oz Pernod

Water

Sugar

---

1. Put the limes into a preserving pan, cover with water and bring to the boil. Simmer until tender, about 40 minutes. They need to be boiled for longer because of the tough skins.

2. Mash with a potato masher, then leave to cool.

3. Strain through a muslin for 12 hours or overnight.

4. Put the jars and lids in the oven to sterilise.

5. Measure the juice and return it to the clean preserving pan. Add 350g/12oz of sugar to every 600ml/1pt of juice.

6. Place over a low heat and stir continuously until the sugar has completely dissolved and there is no grittiness.

7. When the sugar has fully dissolved, bring to the boil and boil rapidly until setting point, about 10 minutes.

8. Test the jelly on a cold saucer for crinkling and, when ready, remove from the heat. If it is not ready, then leave it to boil for another 5 minutes and test again.

9. Take the jars out of the oven and swirl a small amount of Pernod around each jar in turn.

10. Skim the jelly, then pour immediately into the jars, filling not quite to the top. Top up with the remaining Pernod. Put on the lids and leave to cool before labelling.

The jelly will look as if it is runny at first due to the alcohol. After a day or two it will blend into the jelly and will set as normal.

Lemon, Ginger and Cardamom

I love the smell of crushed cardamom seeds, especially with oranges as they blend extremely well. Do be careful not to store them for too long otherwise they lose their pungency. I found some lurking at the back of my cupboard and the smell and flavour had totally disappeared. In general it is better to buy spices in small quantities as they lose their flavour quite quickly.

900g/2lb lemons
1 small root fresh ginger, peeled and sliced
1 tablespoon cardamom pods, crushed
Water
Sugar

---

1. Finely pare off the lemon rind from 2 lemons and cut into long, thin julienne strips and reserve.

2. Cut the lemons in half and put into a preserving pan with sliced ginger and crushed cardamom pods. Cover with water and bring to the boil. Simmer until tender, about 40–60 minutes.

3. Mash with a potato masher, then leave to cool.

4. Strain through a muslin for 12 hours or overnight.

5. Put the jars and lids in the oven to sterilise.

6. Measure the juice and return it to the clean preserving pan. Add 350g/12oz of sugar to every 600ml/1pt of juice.

7. Place over a low heat and stir continuously until the sugar has completely dissolved and there is no grittiness.

8. When the sugar has fully dissolved, bring to the boil and boil rapidly until setting point, about 10 minutes.

9. Test the jelly on a cold saucer for crinkling and, when ready, remove from the heat. If it is not ready, then leave it to boil for another 5 minutes and test again.

10. Skim the jelly and stir to cool it a little, then add the julienne strips of lemon and stir again to distribute the strips through the jelly.

11. Pour immediately into the warm jars, filling to the top. Put on the lids and leave to cool before labelling.

Just Gooseberries

Gooseberries are one of the best fruits for jelly because they have a high proportion of pectin so they do not need any other fruits to help them set. They also make the jelly a beautifully subtle pink colour. Another advantage is that you can add gooseberry juice to other low-pectin fruits. I cook gooseberries and strain the juice into a plastic tub, then freeze it. Once it has frozen, you can turn out the solid juice and put it into a labelled plastic bag so that you have it ready to use at any time with other fruits. The great joy of jelly making is that there is no preparation of the fruits and you can use them straight from the bush.

1.75kg/4lb gooseberries

Water

Sugar

1. Put the gooseberries into a preserving pan, cover with water and bring to the boil. Simmer until tender, about 30 minutes. Leave to cool.

2. Strain through a muslin for 12 hours or overnight.

3. Put the jars and lids in the oven to sterilise.

4. Measure the juice and return it to the clean preserving pan. Add 350g/12oz of sugar to every 600ml/1pt of juice.

5. Place over a low heat and stir continuously until the sugar has completely dissolved and there is no grittiness.

6. When the sugar has fully dissolved, bring to the boil and boil rapidly until setting point, about 10 minutes.

7. Test the jelly on a cold saucer for crinkling and, when ready, remove from the heat. If it is not ready, then leave it to boil for another 5 minutes and test again.

8. Skim the jelly, then pour immediately into the warm jars, filling to the top. Put on the lids and leave to cool before labelling.

Sweet Red Pepper and Chilli

This pink jelly teams extremely well with fish. Place it on the top of the fish before grilling or serve it separately. You can adjust the number of chillies to make it hotter if you wish.

900g/2lb apples
3 sweet red peppers, cut in half and seeded.
3 red chillies (or according to taste)
Water
Sugar

---

1. Put the apples and two of the chillies into a preserving pan, cover with water and bring to the boil. Simmer until tender, about 20 minutes.

2. While it is simmering, put the peppers on a tray in the oven at 200°C/400°F/gas 6 to roast or under the grill until blackened, about 15–20 minutes, but watch carefully so that they do not to burn.

3. Blend the red peppers to a purée in a blender or food processor, then pour the purée into the apple and chilli mixture. Leave to cool.

4. Strain through a muslin for 12 hours or overnight.

5. Put the jars and lids in the oven to sterilise.

6. Measure the juice and return it to the clean preserving pan. Add 350g/12oz of sugar to every 600ml/1pt of juice.

7. Place over a low heat and stir continuously until the sugar has completely dissolved and there is no grittiness.

8. When the sugar has fully dissolved, bring to the boil and boil rapidly until setting point, about 10 minutes.

9. Cut the remaining chilli into small pieces.

10. Test the jelly on a cold saucer for crinkling and, when ready, remove from the heat. If it is not ready, then leave it to boil for another 5 minutes and test again.

11. Skim the jelly, then stir until cooled slightly. Stir in the chopped chilli and continue to stir until beginning to set. Pour immediately into the warm jars, filling to the top. Put on the lids and leave to cool before labelling.

Sweet pepper and apples ready to be made into a delicious jelly.

Lemon, Orange and Rhubarb

Rhubarb is actually a vegetable rather than a fruit but its sweet flavour means we usually think of it as a fruit. It has an uncanny affiliation with citrus fruits and at this time of year there are generous quantities of both. The infusion of flavours in this jelly is delicious melted and brushed over tart bases and then brushed thickly over the fruits.

4 lemons

900g/2lb rhubarb

2 oranges

1 star anise

Water

Sugar

1. Grate the lemon rinds and reserve.

2. Halve the lemons and slice the rhubarb and put into a preserving pan with the oranges and star anise, cover with water and bring to the boil. Simmer until tender, about 30 minutes.

3. Mash with a potato masher, then leave to cool and infuse.

4. Strain through a muslin for 12 hours or overnight.

5. Put the jars and lids in the oven to sterilise.

6. Measure the juice and return it to the clean preserving pan. Add 350g/12oz of sugar to every 600ml/1pt of juice.

7. Place over a low heat and stir continuously until the sugar has completely dissolved and there is no grittiness. Add the grated lemon rind.

8. When the sugar has fully dissolved, bring to the boil and boil rapidly until setting point, about 10 minutes.

9. Test the jelly on a cold saucer for crinkling and, when ready, remove from the heat. If it is not ready, then leave it to boil for another 5 minutes and test again.

10. Skim the jelly, then pour immediately into the warm jars, filling to the top. Put on the lids and leave to cool before labelling.

Rhubarb leaves are toxic but the stems make delicious jelly.

Rhubarb and Raspberry

The colour and flavour of this combination makes a perfect filling for fresh cakes, especially with added raspberries. The jelly soaks into the sponge to give an added gooey texture.

900g/2lb rhubarb
900g/2lb raspberries
Juice of 1 lemon
Water
Sugar

1. Slice the rhubarb and put into a preserving pan with the raspberries, cover with water and bring to the boil. Simmer until tender, about 10–15 minutes. Don't leave them simmering for too long.

2. Mash with a potato masher, then leave to cool.

3. Strain through a muslin for 12 hours or overnight.

4. Put the jars and lids in the oven to sterilise.

5. Add the lemon juice through a sieve to the strained juice. Measure the juice and return it to the clean preserving pan. Add 350g/12oz of sugar to every 600ml/1pt of juice.

6. Place over a low heat and stir continuously until the sugar has completely dissolved and there is no grittiness.

7. When the sugar has fully dissolved, bring to the boil and boil rapidly until setting point, about 10 minutes.

8. Test the jelly on a cold saucer for crinkling and, when ready, remove from the heat. If it is not ready, then leave it to boil for another 5 minutes and test again.

9. Skim the jelly, then pour immediately into the warm jars, filling to the top. Put on the lids and leave to cool before labelling.

Rhubarb and Orange

Did you know that rhubarb is related to the same plant family as dock and sorrel? Unlike sorrel, though, rhubarb leaves are not edible as they are toxic, which is why we only ever use the stems. Sweet cicely and angelica leaves are used for cutting down the acids in sour fruits but if you do not have them, don't worry, just omit them from the recipe.

900g/2lb rhubarb
6 oranges
1 handful of sweet cicely or angelica leaves (optional)
Juice of 1 lemon
Water
Sugar

1. Cut the rhubarb and oranges into chunks or quarters and put them into a preserving pan. Add the sweet cicely or angelica leaves, if using, cover with water and bring to the boil. Simmer until tender, about 30 minutes.

2. Mash with a potato masher, then leave to cool.

3. Strain through a muslin for 12 hours or overnight.

4. Put the jars and lids in the oven to sterilise.

5. Add the lemon juice through a sieve to the strained juice. Measure the juice and return it to the clean preserving pan. Add 350g/12oz of sugar to every 600ml/1pt of juice.

6. Place over a low heat and stir continuously until the sugar has completely dissolved and there is no grittiness.

7. When the sugar has fully dissolved, bring to the boil and boil rapidly until setting point, about 10 minutes.

8. Test the jelly on a cold saucer for crinkling and, when ready, remove from the heat. If it is not ready, then leave it to boil for another 5 minutes and test again.

9. Skim the jelly, then pour immediately into the warm jars, filling to the top. Put on the lids and leave to cool before labelling.

Orange and Thyme

This jelly is commonly served with gammon or cold goose. Just spread it on top of the gammon 30 minutes before it is ready to come out of the oven, when the juices are sizzling and the jelly can melt down into the juices. If you have to use ordinary oranges, add a couple of apples or lemons to the pot for that extra pectin. Remember always to cut thyme with scissors rather than pulling at it or you will remove the roots. For added effect, you can cut some julienne strips of Seville orange rind before you start, then add them to the jelly with thyme at the end of the recipe.

900g/2lb Seville oranges
2 large handfuls of thyme
Water
Sugar

1. Thinly pare the orange rind of 2 oranges, then cut into julienne strips and reserve.

2. Put the whole oranges into a preserving pan with a large handful of thyme, cover with water and bring to the boil. Simmer until tender, about 40–60 minutes.

3. Mash with a potato masher, then leave to cool.

4. Strain through a muslin for 12 hours or overnight.

5. Put the jars and lids in the oven to sterilise.

6. Measure the juice and return it to the clean preserving pan. Add 350g/12oz of sugar to every 600ml/1pt of juice.

7. Place over a low heat and stir continuously until the sugar has completely dissolved and there is no grittiness.

8. Add the reserved orange rind.

9. When the sugar has fully dissolved, bring to the boil and boil rapidly until setting point, about 10 minutes.

10. Test the jelly on a cold saucer for crinkling and, when ready, remove from the heat. If it is not ready, then leave it to boil for another 5 minutes and test again.

11. Skim the jelly.

12. Finely chop the remaining handful of thyme and stir into the jelly as it is cooling to distribute the herb and the julienne strips.

13. Pour the jelly into the warm jars, filling to the top. Put on the lids and leave to cool before labelling.

Orange and Thyme

Strawberry and Elderflower

Strawberries are low in pectin so I add gooseberries to this recipe to make sure it sets well. Redcurrants could also be used with the strawberries for the same effect.
You could use frozen gooseberry juice instead of whole fruit if you have some in the freezer (see page 19) in which case just cook the strawberries without any water, then strain the juice. At step 5, add half the amount of gooseberry juice to the strained strawberry juice; the idea is to retain the strawberry flavour while benefiting from the pectin in the gooseberries to ensure a good set. Elderflowers can be picked in May and June and frozen whole in a plastic bag – this retains the flavour beautifully.

TIP: If you wash the elderflowers, you will lose some of the delicate flavour so use them straight from the bush, just giving them a good shake to make sure there are no little spiders or other creatures lurking there!

900g/2lb strawberries
450g/1lb gooseberries
12 elderflowers
Water
Sugar

1. Put the strawberries and gooseberries into a preserving pan with the elderflowers, cover with water and bring to the boil. Simmer until tender, about 10–15 minutes.

2. Mash with a potato masher, then leave to cool and infuse.

3. Strain through a muslin for 12 hours or overnight.

4. Put the jars and lids in the oven to sterilise.

5. Measure the juice and return it to the clean preserving pan. Add 350g/12oz of sugar to every 600ml/1pt of juice.

6. Place over a low heat and stir continuously until the sugar has completely dissolved and there is no grittiness.

7. When the sugar has fully dissolved, bring to the boil and boil rapidly until setting point, about 10 minutes.

8. Test the jelly on a cold saucer for crinkling and, when ready, remove from the heat. If it is not ready, then leave it to boil for another 5 minutes and test again.

9. Skim the jelly, then pour immediately into the warm jars, filling to the top. Put on the lids and leave to cool before labelling.

TIP: I have a mass of wild strawberries in my garden in summer. I would love to capture their delicate fragrance but they are so small and temptingly delicious that I end up sprinkling them over their larger cousins. If you have more will-power, you can use them for jelly.

Strawberry and Elderflower

Mint and Raspberry

Wild raspberries have been growing in northern Europe for hundreds of years but the fruit has only been cultivated since the Middle Ages. You can still find small wild canes now on wasteland. We had some growing next door to our cottage in an old quarry. What a find!
If you wish, you can make this very fruity jelly without the mint, using just raspberry, or you can add Framboise liqueur for an alcoholic twist. Framboise is a raspberry liqueur with a beautiful dark pink colour.

900g/2lb raspberries
6–7 large stems of mint, preferably Moroccan or spearmint
Juice of 2 lemons
120ml/4fl oz Framboise liqueur (optional)
1 handful of chopped mint
Water
Sugar

---

1. Put the raspberries into a preserving pan with the mint stems, just cover with water and bring to the boil. Simmer until tender, about 5–10 minutes.

2. Mash with a potato masher, then leave to cool.

3. Strain through a muslin for 12 hours or overnight.

4. Put the jars and lids in the oven to sterilise.

5. Add the lemon juice through a sieve to the strained juice. Measure the juice and return it to the clean preserving pan. Add 350g/12oz of sugar to every 600ml/1pt of juice.

6. Place over a low heat and stir continuously until the sugar has completely dissolved and there is no grittiness.

7. When the sugar has fully dissolved, bring to the boil and boil rapidly until setting point, about 10 minutes.

8. Test the jelly on a cold saucer for crinkling and, when ready, remove from the heat. If it is not ready, then leave it to boil for another 5 minutes and test again.

9. Skim the jelly.

10. Swirl a little of the Framboise, if using, around each of the warmed jars to spread the flavour through the jelly.

11. Stir the jelly until it begins to cool, then stir in the chopped mint until it is beginning to set.

12. Pour the jelly into the jars, filling not quite to the top. Top up each warm jar with the remaining Framboise, if using. Put on the lids and leave to cool before labelling.

TIP: If you do not stir, then a skin will form on the top. You want the mint well distributed in the jelly and not a thick layer on the top. When the mint sinks, this indicates that the jelly is cool enough to put into the jars.

Mint and Raspberry

Chianti and Redcurrant

Chianti is a fruity and slightly perfumed red wine from northern Italy and really adds to the flavour of plain redcurrants. You can stir the jelly into gravy to make a delicious sauce to serve with roast lamb. No one seems to know what to do with the little white currants but they do have a flavour all of their own and can be made easily into a delicious jelly.

900g/2lb redcurrants

450g/1lb white currants

300ml/½pt Chianti

Water

Sugar

1. Put the red and the white currants, including their stalks, into a preserving pan, cover with water and bring to the boil. Simmer until tender, about 15 minutes.

2. Mash with a potato masher, then leave to cool.

3. Strain through a muslin for 12 hours or overnight.

4. Put the jars and lids in the oven to sterilise.

5. Add the Chianti. Measure the juice and return it to the clean preserving pan. Add 350g/12oz of sugar to every 600ml/1pt of juice.

6. Place over a low heat and stir continuously until the sugar has completely dissolved and there is no grittiness.

7. When the sugar has fully dissolved, bring to the boil and boil rapidly until setting point, about 10 minutes.

8. Test the jelly on a cold saucer for crinkling and, when ready, remove from the heat. If it is not ready, then leave it to boil for another 5 minutes and test again.

9. Skim the jelly, then pour immediately into the warm jars, filling to the top. Put on the lids and leave to cool before labelling.

Chianti and Redcurrant

SUMMER JELLY RECIPES

During the long days of summer, there is an abundance of fresh produce to be had – just waiting to be made into delicious jellies.

Moroccan Mint and Apple

I have always been a mint sauce addict but having made my own mint jelly using Moroccan mint and cutting down on the sweetness, I now love the jelly too. I serve it as a condiment, or stir it into the gravy.
You can use any apples in this recipe, but cooking apples are preferable because of the sourness. You can also substitute mint with any of the chopped herbs e.g. tarragon, sage, parsley, thyme, rosemary or any other favourite. Chervil is particularly good with its aniseed flavour captured for the winter months. Moroccan mint is my favourite mint for flavour, and to use in jelly making. It is used traditionally for mint tea. Moroccan mint is extremely easy to grow but doesn't have that maddening habit of 'taking over' the garden. It also grows well in a pot, with its splendid emerald green, crumply leaves looking strong and rather elegant in the flower garden.

TIP: You can, of course, use other mints for mint jelly but be sure it smells of mint. There are many varieties now that smell of peppermint or even apple or pineapple. As mint grows in long stems, make sure you cut the stems long as there is lots of flavour in the stem.

Moroccan mint.

1.5kg/3lb apples
600ml/1pt wine vinegar
2 bunches of fresh mint leaves
Water
Sugar

1. Put the apples into a preserving pan with the wine vinegar and a bunch of fresh mint, cover with water and bring to the boil. Simmer until tender, about 20 minutes.

2. Mash with a potato masher, then leave to cool.

3. Strain through a muslin for 12 hours or overnight.

4. Put the jars and lids in the oven to sterilise.

5. Measure the juice and return it to the clean preserving pan. Add 350g/12oz of sugar to every 600ml/1pt of juice.

6. Place over a low heat and stir continuously until the sugar has completely dissolved and there is no grittiness.

7. When the sugar has fully dissolved, bring to the boil and boil rapidly until setting point, about 10 minutes.

9. Test the jelly on a cold saucer for crinkling and, when ready, remove from the heat. If it is not ready, then leave it to boil for another 5 minutes and test again.

Skim the jelly.

9. Chop the leaves of the remaining mint and stir them into the cooling jelly for a few minutes until they are well distributed, stirring continuously so a skin does not form on the top.

10. Pour the jelly into the warm jars, filling to the top. Put on the lids and leave to cool before labelling.

TIP: If the mint is still rising to the top once you have put the jelly in the jars, turn the lidded jars upside down as they cool, which will help distribute the mint. When cooled, turn them right-side up again. If the mint is still rising to the top, then pour the jelly back into the pan and repeat the process. I did this once and totally forgot to turn the jars back again, so all the mint was at the bottom of the jars. They say you learn by your mistakes!

Gooseberry and Elderflower

The gooseberry plant is easy to grow but spiky, so you need to be careful when picking. Fruiting in June, the gooseberry coincides beautifully with the flowering elder (Sambucus nigra), so they are ideal jelly making partners. Cooked together, the juice turns a subtle pink and the flavour carries a delicate aroma of this beautiful hedgerow shrub, creating a jelly that is really delicious on toast or in tartlets. Freshly picked gooseberries are quite unlike those we were served for school meal desserts in the 1950s, which I thought would put me off the fruit for life! The freshly picked fruit is a world away from fruit that emerged from a tin, cold and sour and uninteresting!

Elderflower is a vigorous shrub growing 7–11m/20–30ft tall and found all over the British Isles. The pungent and beautiful creamy flowers are all over the hedgerows in May and June and are easily cut with secateurs.

1.8kg/4lb gooseberries

20 freshly picked elderflowers

Water

Sugar

---

1. Put the gooseberries and elderflowers into a preserving pan; there is no need to top and tail the gooseberries. Cover with water and bring to the boil. Simmer until tender, about 30 minutes.

Gooseberries on the bush.

2. Mash with a potato masher, then leave to cool and infuse.

3. Strain through a muslin for 12 hours or overnight.

4. Put the jars and lids in the oven to sterilise.

5. Measure the juice and return it to the clean preserving pan. Add 350g/12oz of sugar to every 600ml/1pt of juice.

6. Place over a low heat and stir continuously until the sugar has completely dissolved and there is no grittiness.

7. When the sugar has fully dissolved, bring to the boil and boil rapidly until setting point, about 10 minutes.

8. Test the jelly on a cold saucer for crinkling and, when ready, remove from the heat. If it is not ready, then leave it to boil for another 5 minutes and test again.

9. Skim the jelly, then pour immediately into the warm jars, filling to the top. Put on the lids and leave to cool before labelling.

TIP: Elderflower can be useful as a fragrance for cream or sugar as well as jelly. When preparing, do not wash the flowers as this can affect the flavour. Just pick the flowers and shake off any small insects in the flowers! Put the flowers into a jug of cream and leave to infuse. Strain before use. You can use the same process with sugar syrups when you are making a fruit salad. Just put the flowers into the sugar and water in a saucepan over a low heat to dissolve the sugar, then remove from the heat and leave to infuse. Remember to remove the stems before serving.

The elderflower in bloom.

Plum and Rosemary

This is my most popular jelly with a particularly herby tang. Spread a couple of tablespoons of this jelly over a lamb joint half an hour before the end of cooking. The jelly melts and runs down the joint and joins the juices to make the gravy. If you prefer, just add a spoonful to the gravy before serving. If they are available, I get small, bitter Bullace plums, but they are not very common around our fields. The Bullace plum is slightly larger than the sloe and does not have those massive thorns, so it is much easier to pick the fruit. Even with that lovely 'bloom', the soft down on the fruit, don't be tempted to eat them raw as they are very bitter and astringent.

You can use damsons instead or I have even used small wild plums. Ordinary domestic plums are not as tart so maybe too sweet for this recipe.

1.8kg/4lb wild plums or damsons

1 branch of rosemary

Juice of 1 lemon

A few rosemary sprigs

Water

Sugar

---

1. Put the whole plums or damsons with a branch of rosemary into a preserving pan, bending the stems, if necessary, to get them in the pan. Cover with water and bring to the boil, then simmer until tender, about 30 minutes.

2. Mash with a potato masher, then leave to cool.

3. Strain through a muslin for 12 hours or overnight.

4. Put the jars and lids in the oven to sterilise.

5. Add the lemon juice through a sieve to the strained juice. Measure the juice and return it to the clean preserving pan. Add 350g/12oz of sugar to every 600ml/1pt of juice.

6. Place over a low heat and stir continuously until the sugar has completely dissolved and there is no grittiness.

7. When the sugar has fully dissolved, bring to the boil and boil rapidly until setting point, about 10 minutes.

8. Test the jelly on a cold saucer for crinkling and, when ready, remove from the heat. If it is not ready, then leave it to boil for another 5 minutes and test again.

9. Skim the jelly, then pour immediately into the warm jars, filling to the top. Put on the lids and leave to cool before labelling.

A quote from Nicholas Culpeper, the famous herbalist:
'All plums are under Venus, and are, like women, some better, some worse.'
I wonder what he means by that?

'There's rosemary, that's for remembrance; pray, love remember.'
from *Hamlet* by William Shakespeare

Bullace plums.

Rosemary bush.

Rosehip

Rosehips come from the dog rose or Rosa canina, that much-loved plant that winds its way through the hedgerows, bringing out its single, white, scented, blushed flower in the early summer, which develops into the blood red hips in the autumn. The plant grows all over the British Isles and is totally hardy. Dog rosehips are loved by the birds so be careful not to pick them all!

Look for them in the hedgerows after the pale pink flowers have fallen. They are a valuable source of vitamin C and were picked extensively in Britain during the Second World War. Hundreds of tonnes of rosehips were turned into rosehip syrup, which was given to children to overcome the shortage of citrus fruits. It is said that a cup of rosehip juice holds as much vitamin C as 40 oranges.

This recipe is easy but, I must warn you, the picking is tedious. You need a sharp pair of secateurs and a lot of patience as rosehips are not very juicy and so a little definitely does not go a long way. Only use a stainless steel or enamel pan as rosehips will lose their vitamin C and turn black in aluminium or iron pans.

This is an ideal recipe to use frozen gooseberry or apple juice (see page 19). If you are using frozen juice, add it with the strained juice before measuring at step 5, then continue to follow the recipe. Try spreading this jelly on fresh bread and butter or serve it on toast or sandwiched in a cake.

900g/2lb rosehips
450g/1lb apples or 600ml/1pt apple juice
Juice of 2 lemons
Water
Sugar

---

1. Put the rosehips and apples into a preserving pan, cover with water and bring to the boil. Simmer until tender, about 30 minutes.

2. Mash with a potato masher, then leave to cool.

3. Strain through a muslin for 12 hours or overnight.

4. Put the jars and lids in the oven to sterilise.

5. Add the lemon juice through a sieve to the strained juice. Measure the juice and return it to the clean preserving pan. Add 350g/12oz of sugar to every 600ml/1pt of juice.

6. Place over a low heat and stir continuously until the sugar has completely dissolved and there is no grittiness.

7. When the sugar has fully dissolved, bring to the boil and boil rapidly until setting point, about 10–15 minutes.

8. Test the jelly on a cold saucer for crinkling and, when ready, remove from the heat. If it is not ready, then leave it to boil for another 5 minutes and test again.

9. Skim the jelly, then pour immediately into the warm jars, filling to the top. Put on the lids and leave to cool before labelling.

The dog rose.

Blackcurrant

The flavour and aroma of blackcurrants is like nothing else! And you really can't go wrong making preserves out of these beautiful little berries because they always work. Blackcurrants are so wonderfully versatile and are so easy to make into jelly because they are full of pectin and because you have none of the fuss and bother of stripping off the stems. They are easy to freeze so you can have some ready to use whenever you need them. Our family favourite is plain, simple blackcurrant jelly spread on hot toast – what better treat at tea time? But you can try adding oranges at the boiling stage as an alternative; the two flavours mingle well together. You can use the same recipe to make redcurrant jelly.

1.8kg/4lb blackcurrants

Water

Sugar

---

1. Put the currants into a preserving pan, cover with water and bring to the boil. Simmer until tender, about 30 minutes.

2. Mash with a potato masher, then leave to cool.

3. Strain through a muslin for 12 hours or overnight.

4. Put the jars and lids in the oven to sterilise.

5. Measure the juice and return it to the clean preserving pan. Add 350g/12oz of sugar to every 600ml/1pt of juice.

6. Place over a low heat and stir continuously until the sugar has completely dissolved and there is no grittiness.

7. When the sugar has fully dissolved, bring to the boil and boil rapidly until setting point, about 10 minutes.

8. Test the jelly on a cold saucer for crinkling and, when ready, remove from the heat. If it is not ready, then leave it to boil for another 5 minutes and test again.

9. Skim the jelly, then pour immediately into the warm jars, filling to the top. Put on the lids and leave to cool before labelling.

WITHDRAWN

Blackcurrants.

Redcurrant

This is an old recipe I found which uses the 'no boiling' method probably created in the early 1900s. This is designed to give you more of the flavour of the fruit. I have reproduced it as I found it, so I've added some notes to help you should you want to try it.

1. Using the same amounts as the blackcurrant recipe on page 62, put the redcurrants into a large pan and press the juice out of them with a masher.

The original recipe suggested putting the redcurrants a handful at a time into a stiff cloth and squeezing them with your hands, but I think this could be too messy!

2. Strain the juice.

We would strain for 12 hours, or overnight, as usual.

3. Pound and sift the sugar and make very hot in the oven, keeping an eye on it not burning.

Today this would be better done in a warm oven at 180°C/350°F/gas 4 for about 15 minutes.

4. Put the juice on the heat to warm without boiling. When it is as hot as possible without boiling, take the pan off the heat and stir in the hot sugar.

Don't forget to pop your jars in the oven to warm – pots may have been sturdier!

5. When the sugar has melted entirely, pour the juice into the heated pots and seal immediately.

It will turn to jelly or set just as well as boiling but give a richer flavour to the fruit.

Redcurrants.

Rose Pelargonium

I love the pelargonium (Rosa graveolens) for its hardiness and versatility. No matter how I treat it, it still survives and flowers again. Now how good is that? My mother used to make cakes flavoured with these leaves by placing two leaves in the bottom of her baking tin. You simply pour the cake mixture over the top and cook as normal. The recipe is on page 178. The wonderful perfume infuses the cake and if you're very clever you make the jelly to sandwich it together! This recipe shows how the perfume is used as an infusion with an apple base. If you want a sharper flavour, then use crab apples. Rose pelargonium plants tend to get very 'leggy' by the end of the summer, so cut off the branches and use in this recipe.

1.8kg/4lb apples
2 pelargonium branches
A few pelargonium leaves
Water
Sugar

1. Put the apples and pelargonium branches into a preserving pan, cover with water and bring to the boil. Simmer until tender, about 40 minutes.

Rose pelargonium plants.

66

2. Mash with a potato masher, then leave to cool.

3. Strain through a muslin for 12 hours or overnight.

4. Put the jars and lids in the oven to sterilise.

5. Measure the juice and return it to the clean preserving pan. Add 350g/12oz of sugar to every 600ml/1pt of juice.

6. Place over a low heat and stir continuously until the sugar has completely dissolved and there is no grittiness.

7. When the sugar has fully dissolved, bring to the boil and boil rapidly until setting point, about 10 minutes.

8. Test the jelly on a cold saucer for crinkling and, when ready, remove from the heat. If it is not ready, then leave it to boil for another 5 minutes and test again.

9. Skim the jelly.

10. Put a pelargonium leaf into each jar, then pour immediately into the warm jars, filling to the top. Put on the lids and leave to cool before labelling.

TIP: It is easy to take cuttings of the rose pelargonium plant to give to friends – with a slice of cake, of course!

A collection of Caroline's jellies.

Cider

I used my next door neighbour's home-made cider for making this – I'm not allowed to call it 'rough'. The finished jelly has quite a strong 'cidery' taste so is absolutely perfect served with a cooked gammon joint or cold ham. Try it thickly spread in a plain ham sandwich.

1.8kg/4lb cooking apples
1litre/30 fl oz dry cider
A little more cider for topping up the jars
Water
Sugar

1. Halve the apples and put into a preserving pan, cover with water and bring to the boil. Simmer until tender, about 30–40 minutes.

2. Mash with a potato masher, then leave to cool.

3. Strain through a muslin for 12 hours or overnight.

4. Put the jars and lids in the oven to sterilise.

5. Add the cider, measure the combined juice and return it to the clean preserving pan. Add 350g/12oz of sugar to every 600ml/1pt of juice.

6. Place over a low heat and stir continuously until the sugar has completely dissolved and there is no grittiness.

7. When the sugar has fully dissolved, bring to the boil and boil rapidly until setting point, about 10 minutes.

8. Test the jelly on a cold saucer for crinkling and, when ready, remove from the heat. If it is not ready, then leave it to boil for another 5 minutes and test again.

9. Skim the jelly, then pour immediately into the warm jars, filling not quite to the top so that you can top up with the remaining cider.

10. Put on the lids and leave to cool before labelling.

TIP: To make a spiced cider jelly, add a couple of sticks of cinnamon, a few allspice berries and a star anise with the apples at step 1.

Cider and apples ready to make cider jelly.

Vanilla and Redcurrant

A vanilla pod added to your sugar is all you need for this unusually flavoured but quite unique jelly. Simply put approximately 900g /2lb of caster sugar in a bowl with 1 vanilla pod and leave overnight.

900g/2lb redcurrants
1 vanilla pod
1 orange
Water
Caster sugar

Put the redcurrants, including stalks, and vanilla pod into a preserving pan. Halve the orange, squeeze the juice into the pan, then add the orange, cover with water and bring to the boil. Simmer until tender, about 10 minutes.

Mash with a potato masher, then leave to cool and infuse.

Strain through a muslin for 12 hours or overnight.

Put the jars and lids in the oven to sterilise.

Measure the juice and return it to the clean preserving pan. Add 350g/12oz of sugar to every 600ml/1pt of juice.

Place over a low heat and stir continuously until the sugar has completely dissolved and there is no grittiness. You will find that this will be much quicker with caster sugar.

When the sugar has fully dissolved, bring to the boil and boil rapidly until setting point, about 10 minutes.

Test the jelly on a cold saucer for crinkling and, when ready, remove from the heat. If it is not ready, then leave it to boil for another 5 minutes and test again.

Skim the jelly, then pour immediately into the warm jars, filling to the top. Put on the lids and leave to cool before labelling.

TIP: I leave a vanilla pod in my caster sugar jar so that I never have to use vanilla essence (extra expense saved!).

Redcurrant and Mint

This really is best with roast lamb; just spread a tablespoon of jelly over the joint about 30 minutes before it has finished roasting and let it melt into the juices, which you can then turn into the gravy.

900g/2lb redcurrants
1 branch of mint, preferably Moroccan or spearmint
1 handful of mint leaves for the jars
Water
Sugar

---

1. Put the redcurrants and mint into a preserving pan, cover with water and bring to the boil. Simmer until tender, about 10 minutes.

2. Mash with a potato masher, then leave to cool.

3. Strain through a muslin for 12 hours or overnight.

4. Put the jars and lids in the oven to sterilise.

5. Measure the juice and return it to the clean preserving pan. Add 350g/12oz of sugar to every 600ml/1pt of juice.

6. Place over a low heat and stir continuously until the sugar has completely dissolved and there is no grittiness.

7. When the sugar has fully dissolved, bring to the boil and boil rapidly until setting point, about 10 minutes.

8. Test the jelly on a cold saucer for crinkling and, when ready, remove from the heat. If it is not ready, then leave it to boil for another 5 minutes and test again.

9. Chop the handful of mint and add to the jelly, stirring continuously to cool it and get a good distribution of the herb.

10. Skim the jelly, then pour immediately into the warm jars, filling to the top. Put on the lids and leave to cool before labelling.

TIP: You need to ensure the mint disperses through the jelly and does not just float on the surface so keep stirring until the jelly begins to cool.

Tomato and Herb

For a delicious savoury jelly, this takes some beating. The good old tomato is so versatile it can be used in pasta dishes, added to casseroles, brushed on savoury tart pastries or just served as a condiment. A spoonful added to a casserole can totally transform the flavour. Tomatoes have little pectin so you need the acid of the lemons to help the setting. Use the herbs of your choice and don't be afraid to mix them.

1.8kg/4lb tomatoes

4 lemons, halved

2 handfuls of mixed herb sprigs of choice, such as thyme, sage, marjoram, rosemary, chive, chervil and fennel

A handful of the same mixed herbs for the jars

Water

Sugar

---

1. Put the tomatoes and halved lemons into a preserving pan with the mixed herbs, stalks and all, cover with water and bring to the boil. Simmer until tender, about 15 minutes.

2. Mash with a potato masher, then leave to cool.

3. Strain through a muslin for 12 hours or overnight.

4. Put the jars and lids in the oven to sterilise.

5. Measure the juice and return it to the clean preserving pan. Add 350g/12oz of sugar to every 600ml/1pt of juice.

6. Place over a low heat and stir continuously until the sugar has completely dissolved and there is no grittiness.

7. When the sugar has fully dissolved, bring to the boil and boil rapidly until setting point, about 10 minutes.

8. Test the jelly on a cold saucer for crinkling and, when ready, remove from the heat. If it is not ready, then leave it to boil for another 5 minutes and test again.

9. Skim the jelly.

10. Chop a handful of mixed herbs and stir into the jelly as it is cooling to spread the herbs throughout the jelly

11. Pour immediately into the warm jars, filling to the top.
Put on the lids and leave to cool before labelling.

An assortment of fresh herbs.

Rose Petal

Obviously rose petals themselves have no pectin and so in this recipe I am using apples as the base. The vital task is to extract the perfume from the roses. My particular favourite rose is Ena Harkness, dark red and strongly perfumed, which often grows as a climber. I heard in a gardening programme that actually it shouldn't be a climber as it is too big and blousy – actually I love it big and blousy!

---

6 rose heads, preferably dark red and scented
900g/2lb cooking apples or crab apples
4–6 drops of triple-strength rose water (optional)
Water
Sugar

---

1. Place half of the rose heads in a large pan, add enough water to cover them and leave them to soak for about 40 minutes.

2. Bring to the boil, then simmer for 10 minutes.

3. Put the remaining rose heads in a bowl and scatter about 900g/2lb sugar over the top of them. Leave to infuse.

4. Meanwhile, cut any large apples into chunks, leaving small ones whole. Put the apples into a preserving pan, cover with water and bring to the boil. Simmer until tender, about 20 minutes.

5. Leave the apples to cool.

6. Strain the apples and the soaked rose heads, with their water, through a muslin for 12 hours or overnight.

7. Put the jars and lids in the oven to sterilise.

8. Strain through a muslin for 12 hours or overnight.

9. Measure the juice and return it to the clean preserving pan.

10. Shake the sugar from the petals. Add 350g/12oz of rose-scented sugar to every 600ml/1pt of juice.

11. Place over a low heat and stir continuously until the sugar has completely dissolved and there is no grittiness.

12. When the sugar has fully dissolved, bring to the boil and boil rapidly until setting point, about 10 minutes.

13. Test the jelly on a cold saucer for crinkling and, when ready, remove from the heat. If it is not ready, then leave it to boil for another 5 minutes and test again.

14. Skim the jelly, then add 4–6 drops of rosewater, if using. Pour immediately into the warm jars, filling to the top. Put on the lids and leave to cool before labelling.

Rose petals ready to use for flavouring sugar.

Blueberry

Blueberries (Vaccinum myrtillus) are also full of vitamin C. This is a very sweet jelly which I have mixed with apples but you could just use lemons instead. It is delicious on hot scones or toast.

900g/2lb blueberries
450g/1lb apples
Juice of 1 lemon
Water
Sugar

---

1. Put the blueberries and apples into a preserving pan, cover with water and bring to the boil. Simmer until tender, about 20 minutes.

2. Mash with a potato masher, then leave to cool.

3. Strain through a muslin for 12 hours or overnight.

4. Put the jars and lids in the oven to sterilise.

5. Add the lemon juice through a sieve to the strained juice. Measure the juice and return it to the clean preserving pan. Add 350g/12oz of sugar to every 600ml/1pt of juice.

6. Place over a low heat and stir continuously until the sugar has completely dissolved and there is no grittiness.

7. When the sugar has fully dissolved, bring to the boil and boil rapidly until setting point, about 10 minutes.

8. Test the jelly on a cold saucer for crinkling and, when ready, remove from the heat. If it is not ready, then leave it to boil for another 5 minutes and test again.

9. Skim the jelly, then pour immediately into the warm jars, filling to the top. Put on the lids and leave to cool before labelling.

TIP: It is said that pilots in World war II who ate blueberries or their European cousins, bilberry jam, improved their vision and could fly for longer. Blueberries are used medicinally as anti-oxidants and digestion aid.

Blueberries ripening on the bush.

Raspberry and Redcurrant

This jelly has a rich ruby colour and a flavour to match. You are using two very versatile fruits here, which can be used on a multitude of desserts, melted over a pavlova before or after the fruits are put on, or used for glazing fruit tarts. It's even delicious just spread over fresh bread.

900g/2lb raspberries
900g/2lb redcurrants
Juice of 1 lemon
Water
Sugar

1. Put the redcurrants and raspberries into a preserving pan, cover with water and bring to the boil. Simmer until tender, about 15 minutes.

2. Mash with a potato masher, then leave to cool.

3. Strain through a muslin for 12 hours or overnight.

4. Put the jars and lids in the oven to sterilise.

5. Add the lemon juice through a sieve to the strained juice. Measure the juice and return it to the clean preserving pan. Add 350g/12oz of sugar to every 600ml/1pt of juice.

6. Place over a low heat and stir continuously until the sugar has completely dissolved and there is no grittiness.

7. When the sugar has fully dissolved, bring to the boil and boil rapidly until setting point, about 10 minutes.

8. Test the jelly on a cold saucer for crinkling and, when ready, remove from the heat. If it is not ready, then leave it to boil for another 5 minutes and test again.

9. Skim the jelly, then pour immediately into the warm jars, filling to the top. Put on the lids and leave to cool before labelling.

TIP: Apparently raspberry jam is Britain's favourite preserve but the critics say it is not good for the teeth as the pips get stuck in between dentures!

Strawberry and Gooseberry

I have combined these two wonderful summer fruits because they sometimes need each other in a jelly. The strawberry will not set by itself so you need the gooseberry to increase the quantity of pectin, but at the same time the gooseberries give a subtle, delicate flavour to the resulting jelly. The gooseberries are cooked first as strawberries need less cooking time. There is no need for lemon in this recipe as the gooseberries should be tart enough.

This is a useful jelly to serve with any strawberry dessert, and can even be melted and poured over ice-cream. Imagine bringing the tastes of summer on to your table in the cold winter months!

900g/2lb strawberries
900g/2lb gooseberries
Water
Sugar

---

1. Put the gooseberries into a preserving pan, cover with water and bring to the boil. Simmer until tender, about 10 minutes. Add the strawberries and continue cooking for 5 minutes.

2. Mash with a potato masher, then leave to cool.

3. Strain through a muslin for 12 hours or overnight.

4. Put the jars and lids in the oven to sterilise.

5. Measure the juice and return it to the clean preserving pan. Add 350g/12oz of sugar to every 600ml/1pt of juice.

6. Place over a low heat and stir continuously until the sugar has completely dissolved and there is no grittiness.

7. When the sugar has fully dissolved, bring to the boil and boil rapidly until setting point, about 10 minutes.

8. Test the jelly on a cold saucer for crinkling and, when ready, remove from the heat. If it is not ready, then leave it to boil for another 5 minutes and test again.

9. Skim the jelly, then pour immediately into the warm jars, filling to the top. Put on the lids and leave to cool before labelling.

Coriander, Apple and Gooseberry

Coriander is often associated with Far Eastern foods so try this jelly in a curried dish – just scoop a spoonful and add to the sauce. With the spicy flavour of the herb preserved in a jar, it can be used in many recipes from curry to fish. Use the coriander flowers as well for flavour.

900g/2lb apples

900g/2lb gooseberries

2 large handfuls of fresh coriander herb, including the stalks

Water

Sugar

---

1. Put the gooseberries, apples and a large handful of coriander into a preserving pan. Try to use the thick stems and flowers of the herb for more flavour. Cover with water and bring to the boil. Simmer until tender, about 20 minutes.

2. Mash with a potato masher, then leave to cool.

3. Strain through a muslin for 12 hours or overnight.

4. Put the jars and lids in the oven to sterilise.

5. Measure the juice and return it to the clean preserving pan. Add 350g/12oz of sugar to every 600ml/1pt of juice.

6. Place over a low heat and stir continuously until the sugar has completely dissolved and there is no grittiness.

7. When the sugar has fully dissolved, bring to the boil and boil rapidly until setting point, about 10 minutes.

8. Test the jelly on a cold saucer for crinkling and, when ready, remove from the heat. If it is not ready, then leave it to boil for another 5 minutes and test again.

9. Skim the jelly, then stir until setting.

10. Chop the remaining coriander and add to jelly, stirring to distribute the herb evenly.

11. Pour into the warm jars, filling to the top. Put on the lids and leave to cool before labelling.

Strawberry and Redcurrant

May and June is the time for picking these jewel-like fruits. Use the small, ugly strawberries, if possible, saving the large luscious ones for later. It always hurts me when I have to put a really beautiful fruit, especially a strawberry, into a pan to cook. In fact, when I'm doing this I have to harden myself and say 'no don't eat them – they are cooking strawberries!'
There is no need to strip redcurrants. The beauty of making jellies is that there is hardly any preparation of the fruit – which makes life deliciously simple!

900g/2lb strawberries
450g/1lb redcurrants
Juice of 1 lemon
Water
Sugar

---

1. Put the strawberries and redcurrants into a preserving pan, cover with water and bring to the boil. Simmer until tender, about 20 minutes.

2. Mash with a potato masher, then leave to cool.

3. Strain through a muslin for 12 hours or overnight.

4. Put the jars and lids in the oven to sterilise.

5. Add the lemon juice through a sieve to the strained juice. Measure the juice and return it to the clean preserving pan. Add 350g/12oz of sugar to every 600ml/1pt of juice.

6. Place over a low heat and stir continuously until the sugar has completely dissolved and there is no grittiness.

7. When the sugar has fully dissolved, bring to the boil and boil rapidly until setting point, about 10 minutes.

8. Test the jelly on a cold saucer for crinkling and, when ready, remove from the heat. If it is not ready, then leave it to boil for another 5 minutes and test again.

9. Skim the jelly, then pour immediately into the warm jars, filling to the top. Put on the lids and leave to cool before labelling.

Loganberry

The loganberry is a natural cross between the raspberry and the dewberry. I have recently found an overgrown tangle of these tantalising fruits in the garden. They are similar to raspberries but longer and bigger; although not quite as sweet, they are still delicious and rather special. Actually, unless you have an amazing quantity of these berries, I would eat them with raspberries just as they are! Only pick loganberries when they are a dark red/purple colour and come off easily in your fingers.

900g/2lb loganberries

1 lemon

Water

Sugar

---

1. Put the loganberries into a preserving pan, cover with water and bring to the boil. Simmer until tender, about 10 minutes.

2. Mash with a potato masher, then leave to cool.

3. Strain through a muslin for 12 hours or overnight.

4. Put the jars and lids in the oven to sterilise.

5. Measure the juice and return it to the clean preserving pan. Add 350g/12oz of sugar to every 600ml/1pt of juice.

Place over a low heat and stir continuously until the sugar has completely dissolved and there is no grittiness.

When the sugar has fully dissolved, bring to the boil and boil rapidly until setting point, about 10 minutes.

Test the jelly on a cold saucer for crinkling and, when ready, remove from the heat. If it is not ready, then leave it to boil for another 5 minutes and test again.

Skim the jelly, then pour immediately into the warm jars, filling to the top. Put on the lids and leave to cool before labelling.

TIP: Other delicious fruits that can be used in exactly the same way as the loganberry are: dewberry, youngberry (a cross hybrid of dewberry and loganberry), boysenberry (a cross hybrid raspberry and youngberry), tayberry (a cross hybrid of American blackberry and raspberry found in Scotland), wineberry, sunberry and tummelberry.

Loganberries growing.

Apricot

I have included this apricot recipe because apricot is frequently used when recipes need a glaze, so it is a useful jelly to have in the pantry. In any event, it makes an interesting jelly and comes out as a gorgeous dark orange colour. True, I didn't find apricots in the hedgerows, but they are in the markets and can be quite inexpensive when there is a glut in July or August. If you are lucky, you could even be growing your own. Apricot jam is good, but apricot jelly is even better!

900g/2lb apricots

2 lemons

Water

Sugar

---

1. Put the whole apricots into a preserving pan with the halved lemons, cover with water and bring to the boil. Simmer until tender, about 20 minutes.

2. Mash with a potato masher, then leave to cool.

3. Strain through a muslin for 12 hours or overnight.

4. Put the jars and lids in the oven to sterilise.

5. Measure the juice and return it to the clean preserving pan. Add 350g/12oz of sugar to every 600ml/1pt of juice.

6. Place over a low heat and stir continuously until the sugar has completely dissolved and there is no grittiness.

7. When the sugar has fully dissolved, bring to the boil and boil rapidly until setting point, about 10 minutes.

8. Test the jelly on a cold saucer for crinkling and, when ready, remove from the heat. If it is not ready, then leave it to boil for another 5 minutes and test again.

9. Skim the jelly, then pour immediately into the warm jars, filling to the top. Put on the lids and leave to cool before labelling.

Apricots.

Tomato with Chilli and Garlic

This is another great jelly for using in pasta dishes to give the sauce that extra zing! As we all have different tastes when it comes to chilli, you can use more or less chilli according to whether you like things hot and spicy – or much milder. There are so many different chillies, too, so again, the choice is yours.

1.8kg/4lb tomatoes
4 chillies
1 whole bulb of garlic
Juice of 2 lemons
Water
Sugar

1. Put the tomatoes into a preserving pan with 3 of the chillies and the garlic, cover with water and bring to the boil. Simmer until tender, about 20 minutes.

2. Mash with a potato masher – enjoying the strong aroma of garlic – then leave to cool.

3. Strain through a muslin for 12 hours or overnight.

4. Put the jars and lids in the oven to sterilise.

5. Add the lemon juice through a sieve to the strained juice. Measure the juice and return it to the clean preserving pan. Add 350g/12oz of sugar to every 600ml/1pt of juice.

6. Place over a low heat and stir continuously until the sugar has completely dissolved and there is no grittiness.

7. When the sugar has fully dissolved, bring to the boil and boil rapidly until setting point, about 20 minutes.

8. Test the jelly on a cold saucer for crinkling and, when ready, remove from the heat. If it is not ready, then leave it to boil for another 5 minutes and test again.

9. Skim the jelly.

10. Slice the remaining chilli and add to the cooling jelly, stirring until the jelly begins to set to distribute the chilli evenly.

11. Pour into the warm jars, filling to the top. Put on the lids and leave to cool before labelling.

Tomatoes.

Greengage

I love freshly baked bread with thickly spread greengage jelly! These small, yellowy-green fruits are very sweet so can be mixed with a sharper plum for a better set. However, I recommend that you do try making it first without adding plums. When making the jelly, slightly under-ripe fruit are preferable because they have a higher pectin content. In my garden they are great favourites of the birds, so I have to get picking quickly as soon as they ripen!

Did you know that this little fruit was named after Sir Thomas Gage, who bought them to Britain from France in the eighteenth century? In earlier times, they were supposedly found by the Romans growing wild in Asia.

900g/2lb greengages

Juice of 1 lemon

Water

Sugar

---

1. Put the greengages into a preserving pan, cover with water and bring to the boil. Simmer until tender, about 20 minutes.

2. Mash with a potato masher, then leave to cool.

3. Strain through a muslin for 12 hours or overnight.

4. Put the jars and lids in the oven to sterilise.

5. Add the lemon juice through a sieve to the strained juice. Measure the juice and return it to the clean preserving pan. Add 350g/12oz of sugar to every 600ml/1pt of juice.

6. Place over a low heat and stir continuously until the sugar has completely dissolved and there is no grittiness.

7. When the sugar has fully dissolved, bring to the boil and boil rapidly until setting point, about 15 minutes.

8. Test the jelly on a cold saucer for crinkling and, when ready, remove from the heat. If it is not ready, then leave it to boil for another 5 minutes and test again.

9. Skim the jelly, then pour immediately into the warm jars, filling to the top. Put on the lids and leave to cool before labelling.

Four Summer Fruits

When it comes to summer we are spoiled for choice as the fruit is so prolific and colourful, so for this recipe you can use whatever you have in profusion. Colour is the secret here as you are going to melt and pour this jelly over sponge puddings and ice-creams in the winter and you want the beautiful, fruity flavours of summer to stay with you. The choice of fruit is up to you, although just make sure you have at least one high-pectin fruit and try to keep the deep colour.

This recipe would be ideal made in the Vigo fruit steamer because it steams the juice quite quickly, so I have provided an alternative method if you use a fruit steamer.

450g/1lb strawberries
450g/1lb raspberries or loganberries
450g/1lb mixed black, red and white currants
450g/1lb damsons or plums
Water
Sugar

---

1. Put the all the fruits into a preserving pan, just cover with water and bring to the boil. Simmer until tender, about 10 minutes.

2. Mash with a potato masher, then leave to cool.

3. Strain through a muslin for 12 hours or overnight.

4. Put the jars and lids in the oven to sterilise.

5. Measure the juice and return it to the clean preserving pan. Add 350g/12oz of sugar to every 600ml/1pt of juice.

6. Place over a low heat and stir continuously until the sugar has completely dissolved and there is no grittiness.

7. When the sugar has fully dissolved, bring to the boil and boil rapidly until setting point, about 10 minutes.

8. Test the jelly on a cold saucer for crinkling and, when ready, remove from the heat. If it is not ready, then leave it to boil for another 5 minutes and test again.

9. Skim the jelly, then pour immediately into the warm jars, filling to the top. Put on the lids and leave to cool before labelling.

Plums ready for cooking.

TIP: My sister insists this tastes better when you actually squeeze the fruit through the muslin at step 3 instead of just straining it. Okay, it goes cloudy but the flavour is richer and although it goes against everything I've said *not* to do, I have to admit that the taste is wonderful!

Alternative Method Using the Vigo Fruit Steamer

1. Put all the fruit into the steamer compartment.

2. Fill the base with water and put on to boil.

3. Put the steamer on top of the base and then put on the lid.

4. Boil rapidly for about 30 minutes.

5. Unclip the tube to release the juice into a bowl standing below it.

6. Pour the first trickle of juice back into the pan of fruit and refasten the clip on to the tube.

7. Keep boiling for another 5–10 minutes, periodically releasing the juice into the bowl until all the juice has been extracted and the fruit has become a drained and insipid colour. You can now dispose of this fruit.

8. Take the steamer off the heat and empty the boiling water.

9. Measure the juice and place back into the bottom pan. Continue making the jelly as normal, starting with step 5 where you add the sugar.

Cherry and Quince

This jelly has quite a soft set but a beautiful colour – and a lovely flavour. A spoonful gently melted and poured over ice-cream is delicious. Remember, if you have a cherry tree, keep a close eye on the birds when the cherries begin to ripen in June because the birds are always so quick at eating them!

900g/2lb Morello cherries
900g/2lb quince (halved)
Juice of 1 lemon (optional)
Water
Sugar

1. Put the cherries and quince into a preserving pan, stalks and stones included, cover with water and bring to the boil. Simmer until tender, about 40 minutes as they are quite hard.

2. Mash with a potato masher, then leave to cool.

3. Strain through a muslin for 12 hours or overnight.

4. Put the jars and lids in the oven to sterilise.

5. Add the lemon juice through a sieve, if using. Measure the juice and return it to the clean preserving pan. Add 350g/12oz of sugar to every 600ml/1pt of juice.

6. Place over a low heat and stir continuously until the sugar has completely dissolved and there is no grittiness.

7. When the sugar has fully dissolved, bring to the boil and boil rapidly until setting point, about 10–15 minutes.

8. Test the jelly on a cold saucer for crinkling and, when ready, remove from the heat. If it is not ready, then leave it to boil for another 5 minutes and test again.

9. Skim the jelly, then pour immediately into the warm jars, filling to the top. Put on the lids and leave to cool before labelling.

A basket of beautiful quince.

Lavender

This is a highly perfumed jelly which is perfect for using in cakes or fruit tartlets. I think it's a delightful fragrance, reminiscent of old-world charm. I have a friend who is very dismissive about my lavender recipes but he is definitely getting a pot of this one to prove him wrong! A lavender jelly pot makes a lovely gift for sceptic or fan, tied with raffia and a few flower heads.

The flowers of lavender have been used extensively over centuries. The renowned herbalist Nicholas Culpeper, in THE ENGLISH PHYSICIAN, recommends it as a remedy for 'all the griefs and pains of the head and brain that proceed as a cold cause as the apoplexy, falling sickness, the dropsy or sluggish malady, cramps, convulsions, palsies and other faintings'.

1.8kg/4lb cooking apples
2 handfuls of lavender flowers
Water
Sugar

---

1. Put the apples into a preserving pan with a handful of lavender flowers including the stems, cover with water and bring to the boil. Simmer until tender, about 20 minutes.

2. Meanwhile put the remaining lavender flowers in a small pan, cover with water and boil for 5 minutes. This sterilises the flowers.

3. Mash with a potato masher, then leave to cool and infuse.

4. Strain through a muslin for 12 hours or overnight.

5. Put the jars and lids in the oven to sterilise.

6. Measure the juice and return it to the clean preserving pan. Add 350g/12oz of sugar to every 600ml/1pt of juice.

7. Place over a low heat and stir continuously until the sugar has completely dissolved and there is no grittiness.

8. When the sugar has fully dissolved, bring to the boil and boil rapidly until setting point, about 10 minutes.

9. Test the jelly on a cold saucer for crinkling and, when ready, remove from the heat. If it is not ready, then leave it to boil for another 5 minutes and test again.

10. Skim the jelly.

Lavender.

11. Put one or two of the sterilised flowers into each warmed jar,
then stir the jelly until it is beginning to cool and set.

12. Pour into the jars, filling to the top. Put on the lids and leave to cool before labelling.

Guava

This is a tropical fruit that resembles the quince in its aromatic scent and uses. There are different varieties but they are all rich in vitamin C. I am afraid they do not grow in the UK so you will need to look out for them in the shops, but I have made this jelly and wanted to include it for its unique flavour and aromatic qualities. It adds a tropical taste, particularly to cream cheese, so serve it on the cheese board. It is also very tasty served as an accompaniment with duck or goose because of its intense fruitiness. You can try guava without the apple but the set will be softer.

900g/2lb guavas

450g/1lb apples

900ml/1½pt water

4 limes

Sugar

---

1. Put the guavas, apples and limes into a preserving pan, cover with water and bring to the boil. Simmer until tender, about 20 minutes.

2. Mash with a potato masher, then leave to cool.

3. Strain through a muslin for 12 hours or overnight.

4. Put the jars and lids in the oven to sterilise.

5. Measure the juice and return it to the clean preserving pan. Add 350g/12oz of sugar to every 600ml/1pt of juice.

6. Place over a low heat and stir continuously until the sugar has completely dissolved and there is no grittiness.

7. When the sugar has fully dissolved, bring to the boil and boil rapidly until setting point, about 10 minutes.

8. Test the jelly on a cold saucer for crinkling and, when ready, remove from the heat. If it is not ready, then leave it to boil for another 5 minutes and test again.

9. Skim the jelly, then pour immediately into the warm jars, filling to the top. Put on the lids and leave to cool before labelling.

Guava.

Mulberry

Mulberry trees were originally brought to Britain by the Romans, grown as part of the silk trade. The leaves from the white mulberry were the primary food source for the silk worms. Mulberries resemble the loganberry, with their rich, dark colour. They are extremely soft so beware of staining your clothes if you gather them yourself. Once they fall to the ground, it can be a little bit like trying to collect jam, so try and pick directly from the tree and avoid the mush on the ground if you can!
Mulberries alone have a very soft set so they need apples, gooseberries or even sloes to tone down the sweetness and add pectin. The jelly is especially good melted over ice-cream, and I like to add pomegranate seeds for a rich decoration.

900g/2lb mulberries

450g/1lb apples

8–12 mulberries for decoration

Juice of 1 lemon

Water

Sugar

---

1. Put the mulberries and apples into a preserving pan, cover with water and bring to the boil. Simmer until tender, about 15 minutes.

2. Mash with a potato masher, then leave to cool.

3. Strain through a muslin for 12 hours or overnight.

4. Put the jars and lids in the oven to sterilise.

5. Add the lemon juice through a sieve to the strained juice. Measure the juice and return it to the clean preserving pan. Add 350g/12oz of sugar to every 600ml/1pt of juice.

6. Place over a low heat and stir continuously until the sugar has completely dissolved and there is no grittiness.

7. When the sugar has fully dissolved, bring to the boil and boil rapidly until setting point, about 10 minutes.

8. Test the jelly on a cold saucer for crinkling and, when ready, remove from the heat. If it is not ready, then leave it to boil for another 5 minutes and test again.

9. Skim the jelly, then stir until it starts to cool.

Mulberry Tree

10. Add 2 or 3 mulberries to each warm jar, then pour the jelly into the jars,
filling to the top. Put on the lids and leave to cool before labelling.

Ripe Cherries with Kirsch

This is a truly delicious jelly, which is perfect gently melted over a dessert such as pavlova or simple meringues with fresh fruit; you can even spoon it into the bottom of a glass with syllabub trifle. Cherries need a little more pectin to set well, so this is a good time to use the gooseberry juice you have frozen earlier. If you don't have any, you can add a large cooking apple or a couple of lemons to your fruit. You could also use the wild cherry plum instead of the cherries to add a touch of sourness, in which case you would not need to add the apple.

900g/2lb whole cherries
600ml/1pt gooseberry or apple juice
Juice of 1 lemon
150ml/¼pt Kirsch
Water
Sugar

---

1. Put the whole cherries into a preserving pan, cover with water and bring to the boil. Simmer until tender, about 20 minutes.

2. Mash with a potato masher, then leave to cool.

3. Strain through a muslin for 12 hours or overnight.

4. Put the jars and lids in the oven to sterilise.

5. Add the gooseberry or apple juice and the lemon juice through a sieve. Measure the juice and return it to the clean preserving pan. Add 350g/12oz of sugar to every 600ml/1pt of juice.

6. Place over a low heat and stir continuously until the sugar has completely dissolved and there is no grittiness.

7. When the sugar has fully dissolved, bring to the boil and boil rapidly until setting point, about 10 minutes.

8. Test the jelly on a cold saucer for crinkling and, when ready, remove from the heat. If it is not ready, then leave it to boil for another 5 minutes and test again.

9. Skim the jelly.

Cherries with Kirsch.

10. Swirl a small amount of Kirsch around each warm jar. Pour the jelly into the jars, filling not quite to the top. Top up with the remaining Kirsch. Put on the lids and leave to cool before labelling.

AUTUMN JELLY RECIPES

The season of 'mellow fruitfulness' sees the hedgerows bursting with produce that you can transform into delicious jellies.

Crab Apple

The common crab apple (Malus sylvestris)is a small apple growing prolifically in the hedgerows. It is still one of the many varieties of plant you buy as 'hedge plants'. They have been growing in British hedgerows for thousands of years and have been used extensively in cooking because of their flavour and also their high pectin content. The colours of the fruit can vary from yellow to red to bright green but they are always small and round.

You will often see crab apple trees in the autumn, full of fruit and sometimes falling all over the road. How many times have I stopped and collected a bag full – always being very careful of the traffic. The fruit is extremely bitter so don't even try to eat it raw. Crab apples freeze easily as whole fruit and are ideal for jelly making as you simply wash them and pop the whole lot in the pan. Crab apple jelly is excellent served with roast or cold venison. It can also be spiced and served with the cheese board – you'll find some ideas on page 174. Its common name in Northumberland is Scrogg's Jelly; 'scrogg' is a Northumberland term meaning a stunted or crooked bush.

Crab apples.

2kg/4½lb crab apples
Sugar
Water

1. Wash the crab apples thoroughly and put into a preserving pan. Add just enough water to cover and bring to the boil. Simmer until tender, about 30 minutes.

2. Mash with a potato masher, then leave to cool.

3. Strain through a muslin for 12 hours or overnight.

4. Put the jars and lids in the oven to sterilise.

5. Measure the juice and return it to the clean preserving pan. Add 350g/12oz of sugar to every 600ml/1pt of juice.

6. Place over a low heat and stir continuously until the sugar has completely dissolved and there is no grittiness.

7. When the sugar has fully dissolved, bring to the boil and boil rapidly until setting point, about 10 minutes. If it is not ready, then leave to boil for another 5 minutes.

8. Test the jelly on a cold saucer for crinkling and, when ready, remove from the heat. If it is not ready, then leave it to boil for another 5 minutes and test again.

9. Skim the jelly, then pour immediately into the warm jars, filling to the top. Put on the lids and leave to cool before labelling.

'Where the bee sucks, there suck I,
In a cowslip's bell I lie,
There I couch when owls do cry,
On the bat's back I do fly
After summer merrily,
Merrily, merrily, shall I live now
Under the blossom that hangs on the bough'
from *The Tempest* by William Shakespeare

Quince or Japonica

I love the solid, yellow feel of quince (Cydonia) with its unique and faintly exotic perfume. Uncooked, they are very tart and cannot be eaten raw, but they are rich in minerals and vitamins. The flavour is similar to that of pears and the fruit has a beautiful dark pink/red colour when made into a preserve. The quince has a high pectin content and is consequently an extremely good setter.

A dear friend, who has sadly gone now, gave me a beautiful little quince tree, which boasts the most lovely blossom in the spring. It is worth having for the blossom alone but the fruit are exquisite in size, shape and perfume. Dust off the white fluff on the fruit, polish them up and just enjoy how lovely they look in the fruit bowl; any artist would want to draw them!

Because quinces are extremely hard, they take some time to soften, but when they are boiled gently, the flesh is pink and delicious and can be turned into the most unusual but simple desserts. If you don't have a tree, look out for the fruit at the markets in late autumn and freeze the whole fruit until you want to use it. Or, better still, I know people who have them in their gardens and don't know what they are, so look around as you too could be lucky enough to find a tree lurking! Quince will also keep if gently laid down in a cool place. Try one amongst the apples in apple pie or crumble and taste the subtle perfumed, slightly pear flavour.

The flowering quince, Japonica, (Chaenomeles) is a common shrub found frequently in many British gardens. It has beautiful orange or red flowers in the summer which form a seed pod and fruit in the autumn. The flavour is very similar to quince and you can make the jelly using the same recipe.

2kg/4½lb quinces
Sugar
Water

---

1. Put the quince into a preserving pan and just cover with water. They are very hard, so don't try to cut them up. Bring to the boil, then simmer until tender, about 40–60 minutes depending on size.

2. Mash with a potato masher, then leave to cool.

3. Strain through a muslin for 12 hours or overnight.

4. Put the jars and lids in the oven to sterilise.

5. Measure the juice and return it to the clean preserving pan. Add 350g/12oz of sugar to every 600ml/1pt of juice.

6. Place over a low heat and stir continuously until the sugar has completely dissolved and there is no grittiness.

Quince jelly.

7. When the sugar has fully dissolved, bring to the boil and boil rapidly until setting point, about 10 minutes. If it is not ready, then leave to boil for another 5 minutes.

8. Test the jelly on a cold saucer for crinkling and, when ready, remove from the heat. If it is not ready, then leave it to boil for another 5 minutes and test again.

9. Skim the jelly, then pour immediately into the warm jars, filling to the top. Put on the lids and leave to cool before labelling.

TIP: Quince jelly can be delicious served with Stilton cheese or as an accompaniment to game. It is always added to Elizabethan Quince Cream, which is a fabulously simple dessert recipe. You can find the recipe in the chapter Cooking with your jellies (see page 176).

'They dined on mince and slices of Quince which they ate with a runcible spoon,
And hand in hand on the edge of the sand, they danced by the light of the moon.'
Edward Lear

Bramble or Blackberry

Where would we be without the good old blackberry(Rubus fruticosus), hanging black and glossy and so tempting for all who pass by? It is infuriating the way the largest fruit always seem to be at the very top of the hedge, way out of reach for the ordinary human but left to share with the birds – quite right!

The old wives' tale states that when the Devil was kicked out of Heaven, he fell kicking and blaspheming into a blackberry bush; whereupon he spat on the fruit and swore that for ever after we would regret having done this. This is said to be why, from the 11 October onwards, the berries are very gritty and, as my mother used to say, 'unfit for eating, dear; never eat blackberries in October'.

I expect we can all recall happy memories of picking blackberries. I remember I used to cycle up the lane with my son Edward in the child seat and he would lean over to pick the blackberries. I would so nearly fall off the bicycle as it swerved to and fro, while he chuckled with amusement!

This is a wonderful fruit to use for jams and jellies but it does sometimes need a little more pectin to make it set. I have used apples; lemons could be just as effective.

Remember the more sour the fruit, the better the set so don't be afraid to pick slightly unripe fruit. If you prefer, you can add the juice of two lemons to the strained juice instead of the apples.

900g/2lb blackberries
450g/1lb apples
Sugar
Water

---

1. Put the blackberries and apples into a preserving pan, cover with water and bring to the boil. Simmer until tender, about 30 minutes.

2. Mash with a potato masher, then leave to cool.

3. Strain through a muslin for 12 hours or overnight.

4. Put the jars and lids in the oven to sterilise.

5. Measure the juice and return it to the clean preserving pan. Add 350g/12oz of sugar to every 600ml/1pt of juice.

6. Place over a low heat and stir continuously until the sugar has completely dissolved and there is no grittiness.

7. When the sugar has fully dissolved, bring to the boil and boil rapidly until setting point, about 10 minutes.

8. Test the jelly on a cold saucer for crinkling and, when ready, remove from the heat. If it is

Blackberries in the hedgerow.

not ready, then leave it to boil for another 5 minutes and test again.

9. Skim the jelly, then pour immediately into the warm jars, filling to the top. Put on the lids and leave to cool before labelling.

TIP: Remember, if your jelly isn't setting, you can always use it for pouring over ice-cream but test for flavour first before you call it a conserve!

Rowan

Often known as mountain ash (Sorbus or Aucuparia), this small and common but very beautiful tree can be found all around Britain. Many public councils plant rowan because it grows quickly and easily and has an all-year-round prettiness, most especially in the autumn when the clusters of orange berries appear – excellent bird magnets!

The beautiful rowan tree can often be seen growing amongst other trees. The seed is usually distributed by the birds as they eat the berries and fly amongst the woodlands, leaving the seeds behind in their droppings as they fly.

You can collect bunches of berries by cutting off the whole stem but be careful not to pick them in public parks where a council has planted them!

Apparently, in the Highlands of Scotland, the rowan was thought to have some influence over keeping witches at bay and the farmers grew them around their houses for protection.

It is not high in pectin, but with lemons or crab apples it makes a beautiful burnt-orange jelly with a slightly sharp flavour. It is extremely good served with game and rich meats such as goose and duck. I have used crab apples as the accompaniment in this recipe as they grow close to the rowan at times, so seem the natural partner. The lemon juice adds an extra zest and extra pectin. If you don't have crab apples, make sure you include the lemon juice.

900g/2lb rowan berries
450g/1lb crab apples
Juice of 2 lemons (optional)
Water
Sugar

---

1. Put the rowan berry clusters and crab apples into a preserving pan. There is no need to strip the berries. Cover with water, put the lid on the pan and bring to the boil, then simmer until tender, about 20 minutes.

2. Mash with a potato masher, then leave to cool.

3. Strain through a muslin for 12 hours or overnight.

4. Put the jars and lids in the oven to sterilise.

5. Add the lemon juice through a sieve, if using. Measure the juice and return it to the clean preserving pan. Add 350g/12oz of sugar to every 600ml/1pt of juice.

6. Place over a low heat and stir continuously until the sugar has completely dissolved and there is no grittiness.

Rowan berries on the mountain ash tree.

7. When the sugar has fully dissolved, bring to the boil and boil rapidly until setting point, about 10–15 minutes.

8. Test the jelly on a cold saucer for crinkling and, when ready, remove from the heat. If it is not ready, leave it to boil for another 5 minute, then test again.

9. Skim the jelly, then pour immediately into the warm jars, filling to the top. Put on the lids and leave to cool before labelling.

Medlar

Medlars (Mespilus germanica) are a funny, old-fashioned fruit that are not used or even known very much nowadays. The plant used to grow wild but is now probably seen more often in gardens, as they are becoming a little more popular as a small garden tree. I am lucky enough to have a lovely neighbour who, around November, very kindly lets me pick up the fruits hidden amongst the leaves in her garden.

These unusual fruits ripen much later than other fruits, in fact, they need a sharp frost to let them 'blet', or soften, and then you can collect them from the ground. They will look brown, squashed and pretty ugly but the perfumed pear flavour is worth the effort. The younger and firmer the fruit, the lighter the colour of the jelly. Medlar jelly goes particularly well with all game meats, whether it is served separately or added to the gravy.

1.8kg/4lb medlars

2 lemons

Water

Sugar

---

1. Put the medlars and halved lemons into a preserving pan, cover with water and bring to the boil. Simmer until tender, about 30 minutes.

2. Mash with a potato masher, then leave to cool.

3. Strain through a muslin for 12 hours or overnight.

4. Put the jars and lids in the oven to sterilise.

5. Measure the juice and return it to the clean preserving pan. Add 350g/12oz of sugar to every 600ml/1pt of juice.

6. Place over a low heat and stir continuously until the sugar has completely dissolved and there is no grittiness.

7. When the sugar has fully dissolved, bring to the boil and boil rapidly until setting point, about 10 minutes.

8. Test the jelly on a cold saucer for crinkling and, when ready, remove from the heat. If it is not ready, then leave it to boil for another 5 minutes and test again.

9. Skim the jelly, then pour immediately into the warm jars, filling to the top. Put on the lids and leave to cool before labelling.

TIP: Sometimes I cook medlars with some slices of fresh ginger and finish with a few small pieces of crystallised ginger chopped up and floated in the jelly. It's delicious spread thickly on toast.

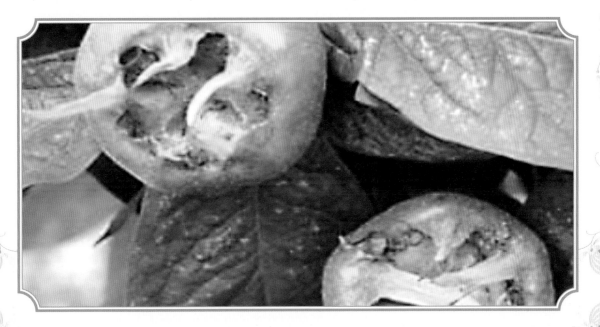

The medlar tree in the orchard.

Medlars growing on the tree.

Garlic

Garlic, with its distinctive flavour, needs no introduction. It has been used for centuries and can be traced as far back as the papyrus records of the Ancient Egyptians, who used it as a remedy for headaches and sore throats .The Crusaders mixed it with animal fat for ointment. And in 1858, science caught up and the anti-bacterial properties of this versatile bulb were confirmed by Louis Pasteur. Garlic has a really brilliant flavour that is so popular. When added to an apple-based jelly, it can be smothered over a joint for the last half an hour of cooking so that it melts down into the juices to make the gravy. It turns your normal Sunday roast into a dish to remember, or can add that wonderful flavour to so many dishes in the kitchen.

1.8kg/4lb cooking apples
4 whole heads of garlic
Water
Sugar

1. Put the apples and 3 of the heads of garlic into a preserving pan, cover with water and bring to the boil. Put on the lid and simmer until tender, about 20 minutes.

2. Mash with a potato masher, then leave to cool.

3. Strain through a muslin for 12 hours or overnight.

4. Wrap the remaining head of garlic in foil and roast in the oven at 180°C/350°F/gas 4 for about 20 minutes until tender.

5. Turn down the temperature and put the jars and lids in the oven to sterilise.

6. Measure the juice and return it to the clean preserving pan. Add 350g/12oz of sugar to every 600ml/1pt of juice.

7. Place over a low heat and stir continuously until the sugar has completely dissolved and there is no grittiness.

8. When the sugar has fully dissolved, bring to the boil and boil rapidly until setting point, about 10 minutes.

9. Test the jelly on a cold saucer for crinkling and, when ready, remove from the heat. If it is not ready, then leave it to boil for another 5 minutes and test again.

10. Skim the jelly.

Whole garlic bulbs

11. Take the roasted head of garlic and squirt one clove out of its papery skin into each warm jar.

12. Pour the jelly into the jars, filling to the top. Put on the lids and leave to cool before labelling.

Autumn Fruits

This jelly is made from a wonderful combination of autumnal fruits. The colour of autumn fruits has always been appealing and the blended flavours make a really useful and unusual jelly. If you make tarts, then what better than this jelly melted and thickly brushed over the top of the fruits? Or serve it in a pretty dish to accompany cold or hot game meats. I usually put a large spoonful of jelly in my casseroles, too, to make them richer.

900g/2lb cooking apples
450g/1lb elderberries including stalks
450g/1lb wild plums or damsons
450g/1lb blackberries or rowan berries
Sugar
Water

---

1. Put the fruits, including stalks, into a preserving pan, cover with water and bring to the boil. Cover with a lid and simmer until tender, about 30 minutes.

2. Mash with a potato masher, then leave to cool.

3. Strain through a muslin for 12 hours or overnight.

4. Put the jars and lids in the oven to sterilise.

5. Measure the juice and return it to the clean preserving pan. Add 350g/12oz of sugar to every 600ml/1pt of juice.

6. Place over a low heat and stir continuously until the sugar has completely dissolved and there is no grittiness.

7. When the sugar has fully dissolved, bring to the boil and boil rapidly until setting point, about 10–15 minutes.

8. Test the jelly on a cold saucer for crinkling and, when ready, remove from the heat. If it is not ready, then leave it to boil for another 5 minutes and test again.

9. Skim the jelly, then pour immediately into the warm jars, filling to the top. Put on the lids and leave to cool before labelling.

A beautiful autumn apple.

'Season of mists and mellow fruitfulness!
Close bosom-friend of the maturing sun.'
from 'To Autumn' by John Keats

Plum, Grape and Cardamom

Cardamom to me is similar to ginger and always gives one the feeling of warmth, especially when combined with autumn plums. If you are lucky enough to have grapes from your own vine, you can use them to make this superb jelly that blends so well with the meats of the season. If not, don't worry – just buy grapes with seeds. Choose the smallest ones at the end of the bunches of grapes as these will contain more pectin.

1.5kg/3lb plums

450g/1lb white or red grapes with seeds

1 tablespoon cardamom pods, crushed

Water

Sugar

---

1. Put the plums, grapes and crushed cardamom pods into a preserving pan, cover with water and bring to the boil. Cover with a lid and simmer until tender, about 20 minutes.

2. Mash with a potato masher, then leave to cool.

3. Strain through a muslin for 12 hours or overnight.

4. Put the jars and lids in the oven to sterilise.

5. Measure the juice and return it to the clean preserving pan.
Add 350g/12oz of sugar to every 600ml/1pt of juice.

6. Place over a low heat and stir continuously until the sugar has completely dissolved and there is no grittiness.

7. When the sugar has fully dissolved, bring to the boil and boil rapidly until setting point, about 10 minutes.

8. Test the jelly on a cold saucer for crinkling and, when ready, remove from the heat. If it is not ready, then leave it to boil for another 5 minutes and test again.

9. Skim the jelly, then pour immediately into the warm jars, filling to the top. Put on the lids and leave to cool before labelling.

Elderberry

The elderberry (Sambucus nigra) is one of the most common hedgerow shrubs. The name, Sambucus, comes from the Greek word 'sambuke' which means 'musical pipe', as the hollow stems were used for these musical instruments. In spring, the glorious cream umbels of highly perfumed blossom are ideal for capturing in desserts. In the summer and autumn, the rich, dark burgundy berries hang in tempting bunches – so get there first before the birds! Take secateurs and snip the whole bunch and then leave them to allow the little spiders to crawl out when you get them home.

During my childhood, I remember as a small, Thelwell rider on my fat lazy pony, picking the elder sticks from the hedgerow. You only had to pick one and the pony would move faster!

The elderberry has been used for centuries for everything from dying hair to cures for the 'biting of serpents or mad dogs' (Culpeper). Straight elderberry is a little drying in the mouth, but cooked with apple it not only helps the set but brings out the flavour and colour. The jelly complements rich meats such as goose and venison. It is also rich in vitamin C.

900g/2lb elderberry bunches
900g/2lb crab apples or cooking apples
Water
Sugar

---

1. Put the elderberry bunches, stalks and all, and the apples into a preserving pan, cover with water and bring to the boil. Cover with a lid and simmer until tender, about 20 minutes.

2. Mash with a potato masher, then leave to cool and infuse.

3. Strain through a muslin for 12 hours or overnight.

4. Put the jars and lids in the oven to sterilise.

5. Measure the juice and return it to the clean preserving pan. Add 350g/12oz of sugar to every 600ml/1pt of juice.

6. Place over a low heat and stir continuously until the sugar has completely dissolved and there is no grittiness.

7. When the sugar has fully dissolved, bring to the boil and boil rapidly until setting point, about 10 minutes.

8. Test the jelly on a cold saucer for crinkling and, when ready, remove from the heat. If it is not ready, then leave it to boil for another 5 minutes and test again.

Elderberries ripe for picking.

9. Skim the jelly, then pour immediately into the warm jars, filling to the top. Put on the lids and leave to cool before labelling.

Sloe

The sloe is the fruit of the blackthorn bush (Prunus spinosa), which can grow up to 4m/12ft high and is very common in British hedgerows. The plant does not always fruit and, like most fruit trees, you can get good and bad years. The fruits are very small and quite hard and are best picked after a frost, which makes them less acerbic. Be careful when picking them as the plant has enormous thorns, but they are rich in pectin and so make wonderful jelly – not to mention delicious flavoured gin for those winter evenings (see the recipe on page 187). Do not try eating sloes raw as they are extremely sour; they are best cooked with apples as otherwise they are quite dry to the roof of the mouth.

900g/2lb sloes
900g/2lb cooking apples
Sugar
Water

1. Put the sloes and apples into a preserving pan, cover with water and bring to the boil. Cover with a lid and simmer until tender, about 30 minutes.

2. Mash with a potato masher, then leave to cool.

3. Strain through a muslin for 12 hours or overnight.

4. Put the jars and lids in the oven to sterilise.

5. Measure the juice and return it to the clean preserving pan. Add 350g/12oz of sugar to every 600ml/1pt of juice.

6. Place over a low heat and stir continuously until the sugar has completely dissolved and there is no grittiness.

7. When the sugar has fully dissolved, bring to the boil and boil rapidly until setting point, about 10 minutes.

8. Test the jelly on a cold saucer for crinkling and, when ready, remove from the heat. If it is not ready, then leave it to boil for another 5 minutes and test again.

9. Skim the jelly, then pour immediately into the warm jars, filling to the top. Put on the lids and leave to cool before labelling.

Gerald Manley Hopkins waxes lyrically about sloes:
'How a lush-kept plush-capped sloe, will mouth to the flesh burst'
Try saying that quickly!

Hedgerow and Sloe Gin

Culpeper talks of the sloes being used as 'marking ink' on linen as well as a remedy for coughs and colds, and gargles for the throat so, like most of our wild trees and plants, this little shrub has been used over hundreds of years for an assortment of tasks.

The white blossom comes before the leaves and fills the hedgerows in spring with a tremendous fragrance. The plant is part of the wild plum family and it is said that it is unlucky to bring the blossom into the house, even though it is so beautiful. Another old wives' tale that you can believe or not, as you choose!

1.8kg/3lb mixed hedgerow fruit, such as blackberries, damsons, haw fruit, elderberry, sloe, rosehip, rowan
450g/1lb crab apples
200ml/7fl oz sloe gin (see page 187)
Water
Sugar

---

1. Soak the hedgerow fruits in the sloe gin for about 12 hours or overnight, covering with a lid to prevent the alcohol escaping.

2. Strain the fruits and place them in a preserving pan with the whole apples, cover with water and bring to the boil. Cover with a lid and simmer until tender, about 30 minutes.

3. Strain the sloe gin and keep it for later use.

4. Mash the cooked fruits with a potato masher, then leave to cool.

5. Strain through a muslin for 12 hours or overnight.

6. Put the jars and lids in the oven to sterilise.

7. Measure the juice and return it to the clean preserving pan. Add 350g/12oz of sugar to every 600ml/1pt of juice.

8. Place over a low heat and stir continuously until the sugar has completely dissolved and there is no grittiness.

9. When the sugar has fully dissolved, bring to the boil and boil rapidly until setting point, about 10 minutes.

10. Test the jelly on a cold saucer for crinkling and, when ready, remove from the heat. If it is not ready, then leave it to boil for another 5 minutes and test again.

Sloes in the hedgerow — you can see the enormous spikes almost as long as your finger.

11. Skim the jelly; hedgerow fruits produce a lot of scum.

12. Pour a little sloe gin into each warm jar and swirl around to infuse the flavour.

13. Pour the jelly into the jars, filling not quite to the top. Fill each one with a little more sloe gin. Put on the lids and leave to cool before labelling.

Sloe Gin Jelly

A Christmas special. Hopefully you will have made your sloe gin the previous year and have some left as it matures. If you have drunk it all, then you can use this year's sloe gin. An absolute must for the Christmas meal with either roast turkey or roast rib of beef, this beautiful jelly looks and tastes equally good as a glaze on your Christmas goose.

900g/2lb sloes
900g/2lb apples
200ml/7fl oz sloe gin
1 handful of almonds
Water
Sugar

---

1. Put the fruits and almonds into a preserving pan, cover with water and bring to the boil. Cover with a lid and simmer until tender, about 30 minutes.

2. Mash with a potato masher, then leave to cool.

3. Strain through a muslin for 12 hours or overnight.

4. Put the jars and lids in the oven to sterilise.

5. Measure the juice and return it to the clean preserving pan. Add 350g/12oz of sugar to every 600ml/1pt of juice.

6. Place over a low heat and stir continuously until the sugar has completely dissolved and there is no grittiness.

7. When the sugar has fully dissolved, bring to the boil and boil rapidly until setting point, about 10 minutes.

8. Test the jelly on a cold saucer for crinkling and, when ready, remove from the heat. If it is not ready, then leave it to boil for another 5 minutes and test again.

9. Skim the jelly.

10. Swirl a little sloe gin around each warm jar, leaving a small amount of sloe gin in each jar.

11. Pour the jelly into the jars, filling not quite to the top. Top up with the remaining sloe gin. Put on the lids and leave to cool before labelling.

TIP: You might find that the jelly looks as if it hasn't set. This is because you have just added the gin, which will gradually infuse into your jelly.

Sloe Gin

Pear and Vodka

I love the beautiful colour and blending of the complementary flavours in this jelly. The exquisite colour is a clear primrose lemon shade with a delicate flavour of pear and undertones of vodka. Simply melt over poached pears for a perfect dessert.

900g/2lb pears

450g/1lb apples

200ml/7fl oz vodka

1 lemon

Water

Sugar

---

1. Put the pears and apples into a preserving pan, cover with water and bring to the boil. Cover with a lid and simmer until tender, about 20 minutes.

2. Mash with a potato masher, then leave to cool.

3. Strain through a muslin for 12 hours or overnight.

4. Put the jars and lids in the oven to sterilise.

5. Measure the juice and return it to the clean preserving pan. Add 350g/12oz of sugar to every 600ml/1pt of juice.

6. Place over a low heat and stir continuously until the sugar has completely dissolved and there is no grittiness.

7. When the sugar has fully dissolved, bring to the boil and boil rapidly until setting point, about 10 minutes.

8. Test the jelly on a cold saucer for crinkling and, when ready, remove from the heat. If it is not ready, then leave it to boil for another 5 minutes and test again.

9. Skim the jelly.

10. Swirl a little vodka around each of the warm jars, leaving a small amount of vodka in each jar.

11. Pour the jelly into the warm jars, filling not quite to the top. Top up with the remaining vodka. Put on the lids and leave to cool before labelling.

Pear and vodka jelly.

Horseradish and Apple

Horseradish can be a devil in the garden because it tends to spread everywhere, so if you grow it for your culinary uses, grow it in a deep pot. It also grows by the side of the road in profusion. The good news is that it is said to keep the 'blight' away from potatoes. Like my father before me, I have to have horseradish with roast beef. This jelly isn't quite as strong as the cream so it might appeal to those with a subtle palate.

900g/2lb cooking apples
1 grated horseradish root
1 tablespoon English mustard powder
Water
Sugar

1. Halve the apples and put them into a preserving pan with the horseradish and mustard, cover with water and bring to the boil. Cover with a lid and simmer until tender, about 30 minutes.

2. Mash with a potato masher, then leave to cool.

3. Strain through a muslin for 12 hours or overnight.

4. Put the jars and lids in the oven to sterilise.

5. Measure the juice and return it to the clean preserving pan. Add 350g/12oz of sugar to every 600ml/1pt of juice.

6. Place over a low heat and stir continuously until the sugar has completely dissolved and there is no grittiness.

7. When the sugar has fully dissolved, bring to the boil and boil rapidly until setting point, about 10 minutes.

8. Test the jelly on a cold saucer for crinkling and, when ready, remove from the heat. If it is not ready, then leave it to boil for another 5 minutes and test again.

9. Skim the jelly, then pour immediately into the warm jars, filling to the top. Put on the lids and leave to cool before labelling.

TIP: If you prefer the jelly to be stronger tasting, put a little grated horseradish into each jar before pouring in the jelly. The root will infuse into the jelly.

Apple and Ginger

For those who love ginger, this is the jelly to make and spread thickly on newly made bread or add to your favourite sponge as a sandwich filling. The lumps of crystallised ginger just add the final gooey touch.

1.8kg/4lb cooking apples
100g/4oz fresh ginger, sliced
4-6 pieces crystallised stem ginger, sliced
Water
Sugar

1. Put the apples and fresh ginger into a preserving pan, cover with water and bring to the boil. Cover with a lid and simmer until tender, about 20 minutes.

2. Mash with a potato masher, then leave to cool.

3. Strain through a muslin for 12 hours or overnight.

4. Put the jars and lids in the oven to sterilise.

5. Measure the juice and return it to the clean preserving pan. Add 350g/12oz of sugar to every 600ml/1pt of juice.

6. Place over a low heat and stir continuously until the sugar has completely dissolved and there is no grittiness.

7. When the sugar has fully dissolved, bring to the boil and boil rapidly until setting point, about 10 minutes.

8. Test the jelly on a cold saucer for crinkling and, when ready, remove from the heat. If it is not ready, then leave it to boil for another 5 minutes and test again.

9. Skim the jelly.

10. Put 5 or 6 pieces of the sliced crystallised ginger into each warm jar.

11. Pour the jelly into the jars, filling to the top. Put on the lids and leave to cool before labelling.

Hips and Haws

These wild fruit look so good on the bushes that I have to try them even though I feel I am taking them from the birds. Pick the rose hips when they are bright red and hard but not when they have gone soft. You need to use a pair of secateurs for this job and it can be a little time consuming! I cook them with apples as they do not have very much juice and limited pectin. The haw blossom, or blackthorn, has a quite an intense perfume and can be used for flavouring syrups but whatever you do, don't bring it inside the house if you are superstitious as it is said to be unlucky!

450g/1lb rosehips
450g/1lb haws
450g/1lb apples
Juice of 1 lemon
Water
Sugar

---

1. Put the rosehips, haws and apples into a preserving pan, cover with water and bring to the boil. Cover with a lid and simmer until tender, about 25 minutes.

2. Mash with a potato masher, then leave to cool.

3. Strain through a muslin for 12 hours or overnight.

4. Put the jars and lids in the oven to sterilise.

5. Add the lemon juice through a sieve to the strained juice. Measure the juice and return it to the clean preserving pan. Add 350g/12oz of sugar to every 600ml/1pt of juice.

6. Place over a low heat and stir continuously until the sugar has completely dissolved and there is no grittiness.

7. When the sugar has fully dissolved, bring to the boil and boil rapidly until setting point, about 10 minutes.

8. Test the jelly on a cold saucer for crinkling and, when ready, remove from the heat. If it is not ready, then leave it to boil for another 5 minutes and test again.

9. Skim the jelly, then pour immediately into the warm jars, filling to the top. Put on the lids and leave to cool before labelling.

Hawthorn blossom.

Haws and sloes.

Apple and Lemon Balm or Lemongrass

Lemon Balm is a very prolific herb growing about 60cm/2ft high in the garden, thick and bushy with a very strong scent of lemon. It is commonly used for lemon tea. If you bruise the leaves, they will give off a glorious perfume of lemon which is why it was used in days gone by for strewing on the floors of homes. Lemongrass, on the other hand, is quite expensive as it is not native to Britain and can only be grown in the garden as an annual. It has a stronger lemon fragrance and is used extensively in Thai cooking.

900g/2lb apples
1 large bunch lemon balm or 2 bruised sticks lemongrass
1 small bunch lemon balm leaves or 1 stick of lemongrass
Water
Sugar

1. Put the apples and lemon balm or bruised lemongrass into a preserving pan, cover with water and bring to the boil. Cover with a lid and simmer until tender, about 20–30 minutes.

2. Mash with a potato masher, then leave to cool.

3. Strain through a muslin for 12 hours or overnight.

4. Put the jars and lids in the oven to sterilise.

5. Measure the juice and return it to the clean preserving pan. Add 350g/12oz of sugar to every 600ml/1pt of juice.

6. Place over a low heat and stir continuously until the sugar has completely dissolved and there is no grittiness.

7. When the sugar has fully dissolved, bring to the boil and boil rapidly until setting point, about 10 minutes.

8. Test the jelly on a cold saucer for crinkling and, when ready, remove from the heat. If it is not ready, then leave it to boil for another 5 minutes and test again.

9. Skim the jelly.

10. Chop the lemon balm leaves or lemongrass and stir into the setting jelly until it begins to cool.

11. Pour the jelly into the warm jars, filling to the top. Put on the lids and leave to cool before labelling.

Lemon balm.

Mixed Herb

Instead of using dried mixed herbs in a pot for your cooking, why not try making this jelly and keeping it for those casseroles and roasts when the snow is on the ground and there are no herbs in sight? Gather together any herbs of your choice and cut them back in the autumn, adding the branches to the apples in the preserving pan. Keep the best leaves for chopping up and putting in at the end, adding several handfuls so you have a really herb-flavoured jelly.

900g/2lb cooking apples
1 branch each of rosemary, sage, marjoram, thyme and bay
1 small bunch each of chervil, chive, celery seed and parsley
1 extra bunch of leaves from each of these herbs
Water
Sugar

---

1. Put the apples and branches of herbs into a preserving pan, cover with water and bring to the boil. Cover with a lid and simmer until tender, about 20 minutes.

2. Mash with a potato masher, then leave to cool.

3. Strain through a muslin for 12 hours or overnight.

4. Put the jars and lids in the oven to sterilise.

5. Measure the juice and return it to the clean preserving pan. Add 350g/12oz of sugar to every 600ml/1pt of juice.

6. Place over a low heat and stir continuously until the sugar has completely dissolved and there is no grittiness.

7. When the sugar has fully dissolved, bring to the boil and boil rapidly until setting point, about 10 minutes.

8. Test the jelly on a cold saucer for crinkling and, when ready, remove from the heat. If it is not ready, then leave it to boil for another 5 minutes and test again.

9. Skim the jelly.

10. Chop the bunches of herb leaves, add to the jelly and stir until the herbs are well distributed and the jelly is beginning to cool.

11. Pour the jelly into the warm jars, filling to the top. Put on the lids and leave to cool before labelling.

Apple, Blackberry and Ginger

This is a version of bramble jelly with the added pep of the ginger. It tastes really delicious served over steamed pudding. Simply put two tablespoons of the jelly in the bottom of a greased pudding basin and tip the pudding mixture on the top, cover and steam. It will just melt down inside the pudding. The advantage of having blackberry jelly rather than the berries or jam is that there are no pips to get caught in your teeth!

900g/2lb cooking apples
900g/2lb blackberries
50g/2oz fresh ginger, sliced
4–5 pieces crystallised ginger, sliced
Water
Sugar

---

1. Put the apples and blackberries into a preserving pan with the fresh ginger, cover with water and bring to the boil. Cover with a lid and simmer until tender, about 20 minutes.

2. Mash with a potato masher, then leave to cool.

3. Strain through a muslin for 12 hours or overnight.

4. Put the jars and lids in the oven to sterilise.

5. Measure the juice and return it to the clean preserving pan. Add 350g/12oz of sugar to every 600ml/1pt of juice.

6. Place over a low heat and stir continuously until the sugar has completely dissolved and there is no grittiness.

7. When the sugar has fully dissolved, bring to the boil and boil rapidly until setting point, about 10 minutes.

8. Test the jelly on a cold saucer for crinkling and, when ready, remove from the heat. If it is not ready, then leave it to boil for another 5 minutes and test again.

9. Skim the jelly.

10. Add the sliced crystallised ginger and stir until beginning to cool and set so the ginger is distributed evenly through the jelly.

11. Pour into the warm jars, filling to the top. Put on the lids and leave to cool before labelling.

A collection of my timeless jellies

Damson and Muscat

Muscat is the famous sweet Italian wine with a pronounced floral aroma; Muscat grapes are some of the best you can buy. I have always loved the sourness of damsons and in this recipe they contrast so well with the sweetness of the Muscat, while the colour is a wonderful ruby-purple.

900g/2lb damsons

300ml/½pt Muscat

Water

Sugar

1. Put the damsons into a preserving pan, cover with water and bring to the boil. Cover with a lid and simmer until tender, about 20 minutes.

2. Mash with a potato masher, then leave to cool.

3. Strain through a muslin for 12 hours or overnight.

4. Put the jars and lids in the oven to sterilise.

5. Add the Muscat to the juice, then measure the juice and return it to the clean preserving pan. Add 350g/12oz of sugar to every 600ml/1pt of juice.

6. Place over a low heat and stir continuously until the sugar has completely dissolved and there is no grittiness.

7. When the sugar has fully dissolved, bring to the boil and boil rapidly until setting point, about 10 minutes.

8. Test the jelly on a cold saucer for crinkling and, when ready, remove from the heat. If it is not ready, then leave it to boil for another 5 minutes and test again.

9. Skim the jelly, then pour immediately into the warm jars, filling to the top. Put on the lids and leave to cool before labelling.

Mirabelle Plum

This beautiful yellow plum grows wild in some parts of the British Isles. Fortunately for me it also grows in a friend's garden, hence my including this recipe as she has kindly given me some of the fruit. Plum jellies can be used with many Chinese recipes and are particularly good with pork belly ribs as part of the marinating sauce.

900g/2lb Mirabelle plums
2 lemons (squeezed)
Water
Sugar

1. Put the plums and squeezed lemons into a preserving pan, cover with water and bring to the boil. Cover with a lid and simmer until tender, about 20 minutes.

2. Mash with a potato masher, then leave to cool.

3. Strain through a muslin for 12 hours or overnight.

4. Put the jars and lids in the oven to sterilise.

5. Add the lemon juice through a sieve to the strained juice. Measure the juice and return it to the clean preserving pan. Add 350g/12oz of sugar to every 600ml/1pt of juice.

6. Place over a low heat and stir continuously until the sugar has completely dissolved and there is no grittiness.

7. When the sugar has fully dissolved, bring to the boil and boil rapidly until setting point, about 10 minutes.

8. Test the jelly on a cold saucer for crinkling and, when ready, remove from the heat. If it is not ready, then leave it to boil for another 5 minutes and test again.

9. Skim the jelly, then pour immediately into the warm jars, filling to the top. Put on the lids and leave to cool before labelling.

The Mirabelle plum tree in blossom.

Thyme and Thyme Again

Thyme is commonly used as a tenderiser for meat so spread this jelly over the Sunday joint half an hour before the end of cooking and then it will melt down into the juices for the gravy. I put lots of thyme into casseroles which need to have long, slow cooking so that it not only helps the tenderising but imparts a wonderful flavour. If you make this jelly when you have plenty of thyme, you can use it throughout the winter.

900g/2lb cooking apples
2 large handfuls of thyme
Juice of 1 lemon
Water
Sugar

1. Put the apples into a preserving pan with 1 large handful of thyme, cover with water and bring to the boil. Cover with a lid and simmer until tender, about 30–40 minutes.

2. Mash with a potato masher, then leave to cool.

3. Strain through a muslin for 12 hours or overnight.

4. Put the jars and lids in the oven to sterilise.

5. Add the lemon juice through a sieve to the strained juice. Measure the juice and return it to the clean preserving pan. Add 350g/12oz of sugar to every 600ml/1pt of juice.

6. Place over a low heat and stir continuously until the sugar has completely dissolved and there is no grittiness.

7. When the sugar has fully dissolved, bring to the boil and boil rapidly until setting point, about 10 minutes.

8. Test the jelly on a cold saucer for crinkling and, when ready, remove from the heat. If it is not ready, then leave it to boil for another 5 minutes and test again.

9. Skim the jelly.

10. Finely chop the remaining thyme and add to the jelly, stirring until the jelly begins to cool to distribute the herb evenly.

11. Pour the jelly into the warm jars, filling to the top. Put on the lids and leave to cool before labelling.

TIP: Always cut thyme with scissors otherwise you pull out the roots.

Thyme and thyme again.

Sweet Cider

I thought that I would experiment with this sweet cider rather than the 'rough' I used before. We seem to eat ham quite often so it is useful to have a jar of cider jelly for these occasions. The orange just reacts in the right way with the cider and gives that tang to cut through the strong flavour of the ham.

900g/2lb cooking apples
Grated rind and juice of 2 oranges
600ml/1pt sweet cider
Water
Sugar

1. Put the apples into a preserving pan with the orange juice, cover with water and bring to the boil. Cover with a lid and simmer until tender, about 20 minutes.

2. Mash with a potato masher, then leave to cool.

3. Strain through a muslin for 12 hours or overnight.

4. Put the jars and lids in the oven to sterilise.

5. Add the sweet cider to the strained juice. Measure the juice and return it to the clean preserving pan. Add 350g/12oz of sugar to every 600ml/1pt of juice.

6. Place over a low heat and stir continuously until the sugar has completely dissolved and there is no grittiness. Add the grated orange rind.

7. When the sugar has fully dissolved, bring to the boil and boil rapidly until setting point, about 10 minutes.

8. Test the jelly on a cold saucer for crinkling and, when ready, remove from the heat. If it is not ready, then leave it to boil for another 5 minutes and test again.

9. Skim the jelly, then pour immediately into the warm jars, filling to the top. Put on the lids and leave to cool before labelling.

Cranberry and Quince

Cranberries can be bought frozen throughout the year. They can be quite expensive but are perfect to use for making jelly. At Christmas time they are much cheaper and are worth buying for freezing. They are full of pectin and so make a very good set by themselves. This delicious recipe boasts the addition of quince. Quince have to be cooked for much longer than cranberries so you need to add them when the quince have been partially cooked. The colour is sheer magic so must be shown off in a glaze poured over the roasting ham or just served as with cold meats as a fruity condiment.

900g/2lb quince
900g/2lb cranberries
Water
Sugar

1. Put the whole quince into a preserving pan, cover with water and bring to the boil. Cover with a lid and simmer until almost tender, about 40–60 minutes. Just before they are cooked, add the cranberries to the pan and continue cooking for another 10 minutes.

2. Mash with a potato masher, then leave to cool.

3. Strain through a muslin for 12 hours or overnight.

4. Put the jars and lids in the oven to sterilise.

5. Measure the juice and return it to the clean preserving pan. Add 350g/12oz of sugar to every 600ml/1pt of juice.

6. Place over a low heat and stir continuously until the sugar has completely dissolved and there is no grittiness.

7. When the sugar has fully dissolved, bring to the boil and boil rapidly until setting point, about 10 minutes.

8. Test the jelly on a cold saucer for crinkling and, when ready, remove from the heat. If it is not ready, then leave it to boil for another 5 minutes and test again.

9. Skim the jelly, then pour immediately into the warm jars, filling to the top. Put on the lids and leave to cool before labelling.

TIP: Apples can be added to this recipe as a third fruit in equal measure.

Bilberry, Whortleberry or Blaeberry

Call it what you will, this profusion of names all point to a small sweet berry very similar to the blueberry, which grows on a plant formally called Vaccinium myrtillus, found on peaty moorland in the north of England, generally around Lancashire. When freshly picked, they are full of vitamin C, which unfortunately is lost in transit as they do not keep well. The larger fruits imported from America have sadly lost the intense flavour of the wild berry. This sometimes happens with cultivation, so take a trip to the peat moors!

450g/1lb crab apples or cooking apples
900g/2lb bilberries, whortleberries, blaeberries
Juice 1 lemon (optional)
Water
Sugar

---

1. Put the apples and berries into a preserving pan, cover with water and bring to the boil. Cover with a lid and simmer until tender, about 20 minutes.

2. Mash with a potato masher, then leave to cool.

3. Strain through a muslin for 12 hours or overnight.

4. Put the jars and lids in the oven to sterilise.

5. Add the lemon juice, if using, through a sieve to the strained juice. Measure the juice and return it to the clean preserving pan. Add 350g/12oz of sugar to every 600ml/1pt of juice.

6. Place over a low heat and stir continuously until the sugar has completely dissolved and there is no grittiness.

7. When the sugar has fully dissolved, bring to the boil and boil rapidly until setting point, about 10 minutes.

8. Test the jelly on a cold saucer for crinkling and, when ready, remove from the heat. If it is not ready, then leave it to boil for another 5 minutes and test again.

9. Skim the jelly, then pour immediately into the warm jars, filling to the top. Put on the lids and leave to cool before labelling.

Bilberries and Whortleberies (inset).

Pear and Sloe Gin

The sloe gin turns the pear jelly a beautiful pink. Serve this delightful concoction with roast turkey on Christmas Day or with the traditional cold meat and bubble and squeak on Boxing Day.

900g/2lb pears

450g/1lb apples

150ml/¼pt sloe gin

Juice of 1 lemon

Water

Sugar

---

1. Put the pears and apples into a preserving pan, cover with water and bring to the boil. Cover with a lid and simmer until tender, about 30 minutes.

2. Mash with a potato masher, then leave to cool.

3. Strain through a muslin for 12 hours or overnight.

4. Put the jars and lids in the oven to sterilise.

5. Measure the juice and return it to the clean preserving pan. Add 350g/12oz of sugar to every 600ml/1pt of juice.

6. Place over a low heat and stir continuously until the sugar has completely dissolved and there is no grittiness.

7. When the sugar has fully dissolved, bring to the boil and boil rapidly until setting point, about 10 minutes.

8. Test the jelly on a cold saucer for crinkling and, when ready, remove from the heat. If it is not ready, then leave it to boil for another 5 minutes and test again.

9. Skim the jelly.

10. Swirl the sloe gin around in the warm jars, leaving a small amount of sloe gin in each jar.

11. Pour the jelly into the jars, filling not quite to the top. Top up with the remaining sloe gin. Put on the lids and leave to cool before labelling.

Pears.

WINTER JELLY RECIPES

In the depths of winter, there are still plenty of delicious jellies to make, and even more warming ways to use those you have stored throughout the year.

Seville Orange

This is a jelly I make for anyone who dislikes any orange peel in marmalade. My daughter always used to pick out all of the peel from my marmalade and so I started to make Seville orange jelly. It still has that sharp and fresh taste and is full of pectin and so sets very easily.

You can easily distinguish Seville oranges from other oranges because they are rather ugly compared to their cousins. Only found from December to February, they are grown in Seville in Spain so we are dependent on Spain having a good harvest if we are to make good orange marmalade and jelly. Seville oranges are sought after by preserve makers because of their bitter flavour and very high pectin levels, making them ideal for making jellies. Extremely bitter to eat by themselves, they are full of pips or seeds and absolutely ideal for extracting juice. Serve the jelly with duck or goose or just on toast.

Personally, I buy a crate of Sevilles from the local market very cheaply at the end of the season and put most of them in the freezer. They freeze extremely well so you can just put them in a bag and take them out individually as and when you need them.

1.8kg/4lb Seville oranges
Sugar
Water

---

1. Put the oranges into a preserving pan, cover with water and bring to the boil. Cover with a lid and simmer until tender, about 60 minutes.

2. Leave to cool, preferably overnight, to allow the pectin to work.

3. Gently crush with a potato masher.

4. Strain through a muslin for 12 hours or overnight.

5. Put the jars and lids in the oven to sterilise.

6. Measure the juice and return it to the clean preserving pan. Add 350g/12oz of sugar to every 600ml/1pt of juice.

7. Place over a low heat and stir continuously until the sugar has completely dissolved and there is no grittiness.

8. When the sugar has fully dissolved, bring to the boil and boil rapidly until setting point, about 10 minutes.

9. Test the jelly on a cold saucer for crinkling and, when ready, remove from the heat. If it is not ready, then leave it to boil for another 5 minutes and test again.

10. Skim the jelly, then pour immediately into the warm jars, filling to the top. Put on the lids and leave to cool before labelling.

TIP: Seville orange jelly makes an ideal present for this time of year. Just add a thin slice of orange to each jar at setting point for that extra wow! factor.

'He hangs in shades the orange bright, like golden lamps in a green night.'

from 'Bermudas' by Andrew Marvell

Frozen Seville oranges.

Claret and Sage

An 'old sage' is commonly thought to be a person of great age and wisdom. I think the two go hand in hand but that's not always the case! In the Middle Ages, the sage plant (Salvia officinalis) was frequently grown as a medicinal herb to use against all kinds of ailments. Plus, it was thought that one would grow to a great age if sage was around. It is also reputed to be able to stimulate the memory! Sage is the mother of all healing herbs. Infused to make a tea and gargled for sore throats, it has a wonderful flavour. We all know that sage is the perfect companion to pork or tastes great in the stuffing for duck, but combined with Claret you can add it to the gravy or serve it as an accompaniment with cold meats for a slightly more sophisticated taste.

900g/2lb cooking apples
1 branch of sage
1 bottle of cheap Claret
Juice of 1 lemon
1 handful of sage leaves
Water
Sugar

1. Put the apples and the sage branch into a preserving pan, cover with water and bring to the boil. Cover with a lid and simmer until tender, about 15 minutes.

2. Mash with a potato masher, then leave to cool.

3. Strain through a muslin for 12 hours or overnight.

4. Put the jars and lids in the oven to sterilise.

5. Measure the juice and return it to the clean preserving pan. Add one-third of this quantity as Claret, so if you have 1.75l/3pt of juice, add 600ml/1pt of Claret. Add the lemon juice through a sieve. Add 350g/12oz of sugar to every 600ml/1pt of the combined juices and wine.

6. Place over a low heat and stir continuously until the sugar has completely dissolved and there is no grittiness.

7. When the sugar has fully dissolved, bring to the boil and boil rapidly until setting point, about 10 minutes.

Sage.

8. Test the jelly on a cold saucer for crinkling and, when ready, remove from the heat. If it is not ready, then leave it to boil for another 5 minutes and test again.

9. Skim the jelly. Chop the handful of sage leaves, add them to the jelly and stir until the herb starts to sink.

10. Pour the jelly into the warm jars, filling to the top. Put on the lids and leave to cool before labelling.

Elderberry and Port

The gentle smoothness of port blends rather well with the acerbic juice of the elderberry. The colour is rich and deep, and looks superb melted and poured over meringues or spread on the base of a cheesecake.

900g/2lb elderberries
450g/1lb apples
1 lemon
300ml/½pt cheap ruby port
Water
Sugar

---

1. Put the elderberries, with the stalks, the apples and lemon into a preserving pan, cover with water and bring to the boil. Cover with a lid and simmer until tender, about 20 minutes.

2. Mash with a potato masher, then leave to cool.

3. Strain through a muslin for 12 hours or overnight.

4. Put the jars and lids in the oven to sterilise.

5. Measure the juice and return it to the clean preserving pan. Add 350g/12oz of sugar to every 600ml/1pt of juice.

6. Place over a low heat and stir continuously until the sugar has completely dissolved and there is no grittiness.

7. When the sugar has fully dissolved, bring to the boil and boil rapidly until setting point, about 10 minutes.

8. Test the jelly on a cold saucer for crinkling and, when ready, remove from the heat. If it is not ready, then leave it to boil for another 5 minutes and test again.

9. Skim the jelly. Stir in about half the port.

10. Swirl the remaining port around the warm jars, leaving a small amount of port in each jar.

11. Pour the jelly into the jars, filling to the top. Put on the lids and leave to cool before labelling.

Redcurrant and Port

This jelly has a fabulous colour and can be used for coating desserts, such as syllabubs and custards. It can also be used as a glaze, melted and thickly brushed over pastries or fruits.

As this is winter time, you will have to use frozen redcurrants but these are readily available in farm shops if you don't have your own supply. Obviously if you are making this jelly in summer then you would use fresh currants.

900g/2lb redcurrants, white currants or a mixture

300ml/½pt cheap ruby port

Water

Sugar

---

1. Put the frozen currants into a preserving pan, cover with water and bring to the boil. Cover with a lid and simmer until tender, about 10 minutes.

2. Mash with a potato masher, then leave to cool.

3. Strain through a muslin for 12 hours or overnight.

4. Put the jars and lids in the oven to sterilise.

5. Measure the juice and return it to the clean preserving pan. Add 350g/12oz of sugar to every 600ml/1pt of juice.

6. Place over a low heat and stir continuously until the sugar has completely dissolved and there is no grittiness.

7. When the sugar has fully dissolved, bring to the boil and boil rapidly until setting point, about 10 minutes.

8. Test the jelly on a cold saucer for crinkling and, when ready, remove from the heat. If it is not ready, then leave it to boil for another 5 minutes and test again.

9. Skim the jelly. Add about half of the port to the jelly and stir.

10. Swirl the remaining port around the warm jars, leaving a small amount of port in each jar.

11. Pour the jelly into the jars, filling to the top. Put on the lids and leave to cool before labelling.

Winter Spiced Plum and Port

This sounds warming and strong – and it is! Delicious served with cold game, you can also add it to pheasant casserole: a large tablespoon added near the end of the cooking. It also makes a richer sauce for Chinese plum pancakes as the plum and port complement the duck. You can use sweet plums from the orchard for a deeper, richer flavour but the set will be less firm.

---

1 orange

6–8 cloves

900g/2lb wild or slightly unripe plums

3 generous slices of fresh ginger

1 stick of cinnamon

300ml/½pt cheap ruby port

Water

Sugar

---

1. Push 6 to 8 cloves into either a sweet or Seville orange, then place it in the oven at 180°C/350°F/gas 4 and bake for 20 minutes.

2. Put the whole plums, with their stones, into a preserving pan and cover with water. Add the roasted clove-spiked orange, the ginger and cinnamon and bring to the boil. Cover with a lid and simmer until tender, about 30 minutes.

3. Mash with a potato masher, then leave to cool.

4. Strain through a muslin for 12 hours or overnight.

5. Put the jars and lids in the oven to sterilise.

6. Measure the juice and return it to the clean preserving pan. Add 350g/12oz of sugar to every 600ml/1pt of juice.

7. Place over a low heat and stir continuously until the sugar has completely dissolved and there is no grittiness.

8. When the sugar has fully dissolved, bring to the boil and boil rapidly until setting point, about 10 minutes.

9. Test the jelly on a cold saucer for crinkling and, when ready, remove from the heat. If it is not ready, then leave it to boil for another 5 minutes and test again.

An orange spiked with cloves.

10. Stir about half the port into the jelly. Swirl the remaining port around the warm jars, leaving a small amount of port in each jar.

11. Skim the jelly, then pour immediately into the jars, filling to the top. Put on the lids and leave to cool before labelling.

Brandied Red Grape

The very smallest and most under-ripe grapes should be used for this jelly because of their high acid and pectin content, especially if you are lucky enough to have home-grown grapes. If you are buying grapes, choose a more acid variety. This is a delicious jelly to melt over chicken or small fowl such as grouse. The juices join the gravy and give the meat a rich, fruity fragrance during cooking.

1.8kg/3lb red grapes with seeds
2 large cooking apples
3-4 cloves
150 ml/¼pt cheap brandy
Water
Sugar

1. Put the grapes, with their stalks, the apples and cloves into a preserving pan, cover with water and bring to the boil. Cover with a lid and simmer until tender, about 15 minutes.

2. Mash with a potato masher, then leave to cool.

3. Strain through a muslin for 12 hours or overnight.

4. Put the jars and lids in the oven to sterilise.

5. Measure the juice and return it to the clean preserving pan. Add 350g/12oz of sugar to every 600ml/1pt of juice.

6. Place over a low heat and stir continuously until the sugar has completely dissolved and there is no grittiness.

7. When the sugar has fully dissolved, bring to the boil and boil rapidly until setting point, about 10 minutes.

8. Test the jelly on a cold saucer for crinkling and, when ready, remove from the heat. If it is not ready, then leave it to boil for another 5 minutes and test again.

9. Add all the brandy and stir well.

10. Skim the jelly, then pour immediately into the warm jars, filling to the top. Put on the lids and leave to cool before labelling.

TIP: A neighbour told me: 'I usually put in a little more brandy than what is recommended, depending on my audience!' Excellent idea!

Spiced Cranberry and Roasted Orange with Cloves

Cranberries (Oxycoccus palustris) are found growing wild mostly on boggy ground, heaths and moors in Northern Britain. Small red-pink flowers appear in June and the red berries follow in August. They are extremely popular at Christmas time so you can buy them easily at this time of year. I don't think I need to 'wax lyrical' about these ingredients; I think they speak for themselves, with their evocation of Christmas, warmth, festive spices and intense flavour.

4 Seville oranges
6-8 cloves
900g/2lb cranberries
1 stick of cinnamon
½ grated nutmeg
Water
Sugar

1. Push the cloves into the oranges and roast in the oven at 180°C/350°F/gas 4 for 20 minutes until slightly browned and squidgy.

2. Put the cranberries into a preserving pan and cover with water. Add the oranges, cinnamon stick and grated nutmeg and bring to the boil. Cover with a lid and simmer until tender, about 20 minutes.

3. Mash with a potato masher, then leave to cool.

4. Strain through a muslin for 12 hours or overnight.

5. Put the jars and lids in the oven to sterilise.

6. Measure the juice and return it to the clean preserving pan. Add 350g/12oz of sugar to every 600ml/1pt of juice.

7. Place over a low heat and stir continuously until the sugar has completely dissolved and there is no grittiness.

8. When the sugar has fully dissolved, bring to the boil and boil rapidly until setting point, about 5 minutes. This jelly sets very quickly, so watch carefully for the setting point.

Spiced cranberry and roasted orange jelly.

9. Test the jelly on a cold saucer for crinkling and, when ready, remove from the heat. If it is not ready, then leave it to boil for another 5 minutes and test again.

10. Skim the jelly, then pour immediately into the warm jars, filling to the top. Put on the lids and leave to cool before labelling.

Mixed Citrus

A deliciously tart jelly to accompany cold meats, this is also excellent on small biscuits with a dry Wensleydale cheese. I have chosen this recipe for winter as the ingredients are easily sourced at marmalade-making time.

6 tangerines
6 Seville oranges
3 grapefruits
Water
Sugar

1. Put the tangerines and oranges into a preserving pan with the halved grapefruits, cover with water and bring to the boil. Cover with a lid and simmer until tender, about 60 minutes.

2. Mash with a potato masher, then leave to cool.

3. Strain through a muslin for 12 hours or overnight.

4. Put the jars and lids in the oven to sterilise.

5. Measure the juice and return it to the clean preserving pan. Add 350g/12oz of sugar to every 600ml/1pt of juice.

6. Place over a low heat and stir continuously until the sugar has completely dissolved and there is no grittiness.

7. When the sugar has fully dissolved, bring to the boil and boil rapidly until setting point, about 10 minutes.

8. Test the jelly on a cold saucer for crinkling and, when ready, remove from the heat. If it is not ready, then leave it to boil for another 5 minutes and test again.

9. Skim the jelly, then pour immediately into the warm jars, filling to the top. Put on the lids and leave to cool before labelling.

TIP: As an additional option, you can thinly cut into julienne strips the cooked and pared citrus skins of two of the fruits and stir them into the jelly near the end of boiling at step 7. so they are thoroughly cooked.

Mixed citrus jelly.

Blackcurrant and Curaçao

The wonderful acidic fragrance of this tough little fruit makes it easy to use for so many desserts. The explosion of colour when it's mashed, not to mention the amount of pectin it holds, makes it the ideal fruit for jams and jellies. I have used Curaçao here as orange is one of the flavours that blend so well with blackcurrant but experiment with other liqueurs as there are no hard and fast rules.

900g/2lb blackcurrants
120ml/4fl oz Curaçao
Juice of 1 lemon (optional)
Water
Sugar

1. Put the blackcurrants with their stalks into a preserving pan, cover with water and bring to the boil. Cover with a lid and simmer until tender, about 20 minutes.

2. Mash with a potato masher, then leave to cool.

3. Strain through a muslin for 12 hours or overnight.

4. Put the jars and lids in the oven to sterilise.

5. Add the lemon juice, if using, through a sieve to the strained juice. Measure the juice and return it to the clean preserving pan. Add 350g/12oz of sugar to every 600ml/1pt of juice.

6. Place over a low heat and stir continuously until the sugar has completely dissolved and there is no grittiness.

7. When the sugar has fully dissolved, bring to the boil and boil rapidly until setting point, about 10 minutes.

8. Test the jelly on a cold saucer for crinkling and, when ready, remove from the heat. If it is not ready, then leave it to boil for another 5 minutes and test again.

9. Swirl a little of the Curaçao around each of the warmed jars, leaving a small amount of Curaçao in each jar.

10. Skim the jelly, then pour immediately into the jars, filling to the top. Put on the lids and leave to cool before labelling.

Tangerine and Cardamon

The intense fragrance of the cardamom seeds crushed with the tangerines, entangled with the sourness of the limes, gives this jelly a real Christmas feel. It can be melted and poured over ice-cream or pavlova, or even used as a glaze over duck, roasted in the oven and mixed into the juices of the gravy.

900g/2lb tangerines

2 limes

10 cardamom seeds, crushed

Water

Sugar

---

1. Thinly pare the rind from the tangerines, cut into fine julienne strips and reserve.

2. Put the tangerines and limes into a preserving pan with the crushed cardamom seeds, cover with water and bring to the boil. Cover with a lid and simmer until tender, about 40 minutes.

3. Mash with a potato masher, then leave to cool.

4. Strain through a muslin for 12 hours or overnight.

5. Put the jars and lids in the oven to sterilise.

6. Measure the juice and return it to the clean preserving pan. Add 350g/12oz of sugar to every 600ml/1pt of juice. Add the julienne strips of rind.

7. Place over a low heat and stir continuously until the sugar has completely dissolved and there is no grittiness.

8. When the sugar has fully dissolved, bring to the boil and boil rapidly until setting point, about 10 minutes.

9. Test the jelly on a cold saucer for crinkling and, when ready, remove from the heat. If it is not ready, then leave it to boil for another 5 minutes and test again.

10. Skim the jelly, then pour immediately into the warm jars, filling to the top. Put on the lids and leave to cool before labelling.

Kumquat and Seville

Kumquats are small orange fruits found in the shops around Christmas and are extremely versatile as they can be eaten whole or sliced and put into salads, even served on top of ice-cream. Kumquats are thought to have come from China where they were known as kam kwat. This jelly, with its slightly acidic, fruity taste, is delicious used in pastry tarts for sealing the pastry and then glazing the top of the pastry or fruits. A puréed apple tart with sliced kumquats scattered in the apple pulp, cooked in the oven, left to cool and then glazed with this fruity jelly makes a wonderful, wintry Sunday lunch finale.

900g/2lb Seville oranges
450gm/1lb kumquats
Water
Sugar

1. Put all the whole fruit into a preserving pan, cover with water and bring to the boil. Cover with a lid and simmer until tender, about 40 minutes.

2. Remove 6 or 7 whole kumquats for decoration. Mash the remaining mixture with a potato masher, then leave to cool.

3. Strain through a muslin for 12 hours or overnight.

4. Put the jars and lids in the oven to sterilise.

5. Measure the juice and return it to the clean preserving pan. Add 350g/12oz of sugar to every 600ml/1pt of juice.

6. Place over a low heat and stir continuously until the sugar has completely dissolved and there is no grittiness.

7. When the sugar has fully dissolved, bring to the boil and boil rapidly until setting point, about 10 minutes.

8. Test the jelly on a cold saucer for crinkling and, when ready, remove from the heat. If it is not ready, then leave it to boil for another 5 minutes and test again.

9. Place a whole kumquat in each warm jar.

10. Skim the jelly, then pour immediately into the jars, filling to the top. Put on the lids and leave to cool before labelling.

Prune and Port

The very best prunes, or dried plums, come from France in the Agen, where they are famous for both their size and for being soaked in Armagnac, which is a local speciality. Leave the stones in when you boil the fruit and they both improve the setting qualities and impart a subtle flavour of almonds.

500g/18oz prunes with stones
6 to 7 extra prunes
450g/1lb cooking apples
300 ml/½pt cheap ruby port
Water
Sugar

1. Put 6–7 prunes to soak in the port.

2. Soak the remaining prunes in enough water to cover for about 60 minutes to swell the fruit.

3. Tip the prunes and the soaking water into a preserving pan, add the apples, then add enough extra water to cover the fruit. Bring to the boil, cover with a lid and simmer until tender, about 20 minutes.

4. Mash with a potato masher, then leave to cool.

5. Strain through a muslin for 12 hours or overnight.

6. Put the jars and lids in the oven to sterilise.

7. Measure the juice and return it to the clean preserving pan. Add 350g/12oz of sugar to every 600ml/1pt of juice.

8. Place over a low heat and stir continuously until the sugar has completely dissolved and there is no grittiness.

9. When the sugar has fully dissolved, bring to the boil and boil rapidly until setting point, about 10 minutes.

10. Test the jelly on a cold saucer for crinkling and, when ready, remove from the heat. If it is not ready, then leave it to boil for another 5 minutes and test again.

11. Remove the prunes from the port and take out the stones.

12. Swirl a little of the port around each of the warmed jars and pop in a soaked prune, then stir the remaining port into the jelly.

13. Skim the jelly, then stir to allow it to cool a little before pouring it into the jars, filling to the top. Put on the lids and leave to cool before labelling.

Prune and Port

Grapefruit and Clementine

The tarty tang of grapefruit blends rather well with the sweetness of the smallest of the tangerine family. Make this jelly when there is a glut of citrus fruits around January and put a spoonful into a game casserole. It also goes rather well with Chinese foods, especially in sweet and sour dishes.

4 grapefruits

6 clementines

1 lemon

Water

Sugar

1. Halve the grapefruit and put into a preserving pan with the clementines and lemons, cover with water and bring to the boil. Cover with a lid and simmer until tender, about 40 minutes.

2. Mash with a potato masher, then leave to cool.

3. Strain through a muslin for 12 hours or overnight.

4. Put the jars and lids in the oven to sterilise.

5. Measure the juice and return it to the clean preserving pan. Add 350g/12oz of sugar to every 600ml/1pt of juice.

6. Place over a low heat and stir continuously until the sugar has completely dissolved and there is no grittiness.

7. When the sugar has fully dissolved, bring to the boil and boil rapidly until setting point, about 10 minutes.

8. Test the jelly on a cold saucer for crinkling and, when ready, remove from the heat. If it is not ready, then leave it to boil for another 5 minutes and test again.

9. Skim the jelly, then pour immediately into the warm jars, filling to the top. Put on the lids and leave to cool before labelling.

Baked Apple and Date

This recipe is designed for Vigo's Mehu-Liisa fruit steamer. Have you ever craved a spicy baked apple stuffed with dates and sugar as comfort food on a winter's evening? Baked apples and baked potatoes are my ultimate comfort foods in the cold winter months. So why not make a jelly that tastes just like that and spread it on hot toast or melt it over the apples for a tastier crumble.

I am making this in the Vigo fruit steamer, but it can just as easily be made in the normal way by placing the baked apples in a preserving pan with about 600ml/1pt of water, plus the water they have been poached in, and boiled for 5 minutes. You do not need very long cooking because the apples with the spices have already been cooked. Mash and proceed in the same way, straining them through the muslin.

---

4 large cooking apples

8 dried dates

4 teaspoons mixed spice

Water

Sugar

---

1. Core the apples and make a horizontal cut around the centre to prevent the skin from bursting. Mix the dates with the mixed spice and use to stuff the centre of the apples. Place in an ovenproof dish and add enough water to come half way up the apples.

2. Put into the oven at 180°C/350°F/gas 4 until tender, about 30 minutes.

3. Remove from the oven and pour into the Vigo fruit steamer.

4. Boil rapidly until the juice is extracted via the special pipe at the base of the steamer.

5. Put the jars and lids in the oven to sterilise.

6. Measure the juice and return it to the empty bottom part of the steamer.

7. Add 350g/12oz of granulated sugar to every 600 ml/1pt of juice and simmer on a low heat, stirring continuously over the heat to make sure that the sugar has dissolved and there is no grittiness.

8. When the sugar has fully dissolved, bring to the boil and boil rapidly until setting point, about 10 minutes.

9. Test the jelly on a cold saucer for crinkling and, when ready, remove from the heat. If it is not ready, then leave it to boil for another 5 minutes and test again.

10. Skim the jelly, then and pour into the warm jars, filling to the top. Put on the lids and leave to cool before labelling.

Late Nineteenth-century Spiced Crab Apple

This is another old recipe from my lovely friend's grandmother. It just shows us how, over the years, neither the ingredients nor the recipes have changed very much – perhaps just the technology! This is a wonderful jelly warmed and brushed on top of many apple puddings, including one of my favourites, the delicious French open apple flan.

900g/2lb crab apples
1 stick of cinnamon
½ grated nutmeg
1 dessertspoon cloves
Water
Sugar

1. Put the apples, cinnamon, nutmeg and half the cloves into a preserving pan, cover with water and bring to the boil. Cover with a lid and simmer until tender, about 20 minutes.

2. Mash with a potato masher, then leave to cool.

3. Strain through a muslin for 12 hours or overnight.

4. Put the jars and lids in the oven to sterilise.

5. Measure the juice and return it to the clean preserving pan. Add 350g/12oz of sugar to every 600ml/1pt of juice.

6. Place over a low heat and stir continuously until the sugar has completely dissolved and there is no grittiness.

7. When the sugar has fully dissolved, bring to the boil and boil rapidly until setting point, about 10 minutes.

8. Test the jelly on a cold saucer for crinkling and, when ready, remove from the heat. If it is not ready, then leave it to boil for another 5 minutes and test again.

9. Skim the jelly, and stir until it is beginning to cool.

10. Put 2 or 3 cloves into each warm jar, then pour in the jelly, filling to the top. Put on the lids and leave to cool before labelling.

Variations on a Theme

Here are some different ways to change the flavours of your fruit to your particular taste.

Just a few of the herbs and spices you can use in your jellies.

Flavourings

If you want to alter the flavour of a jelly, perhaps for Christmas, here are a few variations to add to your basic recipe.

For a Spiced Jelly

Choose from the following and always use whole spices because they hold their flavour better; never be tempted to use powdered spices. Add the spices at the beginning of cooking.

1 stick of cinnamon.
6–10 cloves.
1 tablespoon of allspice berries.
2–3 star anise.
A few slices of fresh ginger.

TIP: Remember that whatever you add to the cooking fruit will be strained through the muslin and only the flavour comes through, so there's no complicated preparation.

For Something Hot and Spicy

Choose from these flavours. There are so many different kinds of chilli, you must be guided by your own taste in terms of type and quantity; just remember, the smaller they are, the hotter they are likely to be. Add chillies or ginger to the cooking fruit, or add crystallised ginger at the setting stage.

2–3 chillies.
3–4 slices of fresh ginger.
A spoonful of chopped crystallised ginger.

For Something Herby

Add a large bunch of your favourite herbs with the cooking fruit, then stir some chopped leaves into the finished jelly.

TIP: If you are adding chopped herbs, then you need a little more patience and time. At setting stage, stir the jelly until it has cooled a little, remove the scum with the skimming spoon and add the chopped herbs. Continue stirring until you can see the herbs floating to the bottom. This is to distribute the herbs evenly through the jelly. Pour the jelly into the warmed jars. If the herbs are still floating to the top, then pour the jelly back into the pan and stir a little more to cool.

For Fragrant Flavours

Add your chosen stems to the cooking fruit at the beginning of the recipe, then at setting point add 1 or 2 leaves to each jar, or a flower, if you prefer. Be careful how much lavender you use as the taste is very strong.

2–3 stems of pelargonium.
2–3 twigs of lavender.

Adding Infusions

Try making simple apple or gooseberry jelly and adding infusions of:

Coriander.
Elderflower.
Jasmine.
Lavender.
Lemon verbena.
Lemongrass.
Rose petals.

To make an infusion, simply pour boiling water over the herbs and leave to cool, then strain.

Less Common Fruits for Jelly Making

I have mentioned wild fruits that I have found around the south of England but there are others that are found in different parts of the British Isles, some of which are plentiful and others not. These can be used in exactly the same way as all the other wild berries but you will have to do the pectin test to see how good each one is for setting.

All these wild berries can be turned into jelly in exactly the same way as the barberry recipe below.

Barberry

Barberries are among England's forgotten fruits, probably because they are very acid and cannot be eaten raw. In the seventeenth century, they were candied in bunches or preserved in jams and jellies. Nowadays they are used in curries instead of tamarinds.

900g/2lb barberries

Water

Sugar

1. Slightly bruise the fruit and put them into a preserving pan, cover with water and bring to the boil. Cover with a lid and simmer until tender, about 10 minutes.

2. Mash with a potato masher, then leave to cool.

3. Strain through a muslin for 12 hours or overnight.

4. Put the jars and lids in the oven to sterilise.

5. Measure the juice and return it to the clean preserving pan. Add 350g/12oz of sugar to every 600ml/1pt of juice.

6. Place over a low heat and stir continuously until the sugar has completely dissolved and there is no grittiness.

7. When the sugar has fully dissolved, bring to the boil and boil rapidly until setting point, about 10 minutes.

8. Test the jelly on a cold saucer for crinkling and, when ready, remove from the heat. If it is not ready, then leave it to boil for another 5 minutes and test again.

9. Skim the jelly, then pour immediately into the warm jars, filling to the top. Put on the lids and leave to cool before labelling.

Bearberry

The bearberry plant (*Arctostaphylos uva-ursi*) has trailing, shiny, evergreen leaves, pink-tipped flowers in June and red berries. It is found on stony moors in Scotland and the west of Ireland.

Barberries

Bearberries.

Bilberry, whortleberry, blaeberry

I included a recipe for this berry (*Vaccinum myrtilus*) on page 142. It is only found very occasionally in south-east England, East Anglia and the Midlands but more commonly grows on northern and Scottish moorland. It flowers from April to June and the berries are black with a blue blush.

Cowberry

This small evergreen bush (*Vaccinium vitis idaea*) with leathery leaves is found on peat moors North Wales and Ireland. It flowers from May to July and boasts beautiful scarlet berries.

Crowberry

Found on moorland in Scotland and also in north and west England as far south as Devon, the Crowberry (*Empetrum nigrum*) has prostrate stems that blossom with mostly pink flowers in May and June.

Crowberry.

Tropical Fruits for Jelly Making

There are many tropical fruits which we do not grow in Britain but you can buy easily. I have named just a few that I have used or know about from overseas. Apart from the kiwi fruit, experiment with different fruits for your jellies and remember to do the pectin test on page 20 to help you to work out whether the fruit will set. If the fruit is low in pectin, just add some juice from a high-pectin fruit and follow the basic jelly recipe.

Hoy plums: Known as Jamaican plum they are, in fact, from the mango family, from a tree producing juicy and fragrant fruit that is used for Indian recipes.

Kiwi fruit: This familiar little fruit is the one NOT to use as the enzymes in the fruit prevent gelatine of any sort from setting. That's a shame as it's such a common fruit nowadays.

Loquats: From China originally, and part of the apple/pear family, these are sandy-coloured fruits and resemble the more commonly known lychee.

Passion fruit: I use these dried-up looking fruits with orange as they make a deliciously fragrant dessert or jelly.

Physallis: Commonly known as a Cape gooseberry, this is grown in Britain for the bright orange lanterns that brighten up the house when dried in the winter. It has golden berries around September that make an interesting jelly.

Pomegranate: A strange ball-like fruit, inside are small jewel-like beads which, when knocked, come out of the husk. Pomegranate can make a beautiful pink jelly, which is generally found around Christmas time.

Prickly pears: The fruit of the cactus, this is extremely difficult to peel because of its prickles but delicious to eat.

Tamarillos: Commonly known as the tree tomato as it resembles a common tomato hanging from a tree, this large fruit has a bright red skin and black seeds.

Cooking with your Jellies – Some Traditional Recipes

Now you have a store of wonderful jellies, here are some more ideas on how you can use them in your cooking, plus a few fruity recipes that will be indispensible in your kitchen – like sloe gin! They include some of my favourites. The recipes serve four.

Gravies

I can't imagine being without a choice of jellies to add to that slightly tasteless gravy. I just add a spoonful of a flavoursome jelly that will complement the meat. Here are some good combinations.

- Plum and rosemary jelly over lamb.
- Mint for roast lamb.
- Sage and port with the venison or game.
- Crab apple for roast pork.
- Garlic jelly for roast beef.

Any of these jellies can also be spooned over the joint half an hour before it is ready, so that the jelly melts down into the fats and can be used naturally in the gravy. Or pop a spoonful into the pan when you are finishing pan-fried meats.

Just Jelly with Cold Meats

- Serve jellies as a condiment with cold meats.
- Rowan with duck.
- Quince with Stilton cheese or with ham.
- Elderberry and redcurrant with lamb and venison.

Glazing Tarts and Filling Cakes

I've included a complete tart recipe in this chapter so that you can use your jellies to reproduce those wonderful, shiny fruit tartlets you see in the French and Italian patisserie windows. Simply put 1–2 tablespoons of jelly into a small pan and melt on low heat. Using a pastry brush, paint the jelly over the fruits tart very thickly and leave to cool. Glaze is also used for sealing the pastry from the juices of the fruit, so brush the pastry before the fruit is added.

You can also use jellies of all kinds to sandwich cakes together – any sweet flavour will work, but I have included a recipe for my particular favourite, rose pelargonium sandwich cake. Another good jelly to use is elderflower and gooseberry.

You can also use jellies instead of butter icing to make what our mothers called 'butterfly' cakes.

Hot Drinks

Pour boiling water over a spoonful of blackberry, blackcurrant or redcurrant jelly in a mug and add the juice of a lemon – a great remedy for a cold.

Presents

Instead of the ubiquitous box of chocolates, I always take a pot of home-made jelly or marmalade to friends. I often swap with friends who have made different recipes – it's fun to exchange ideas!

Lamb Shrewsbury

This is a deliciously sweet main course prepared quickly and easily using redcurrant or quince jelly. It can be made ahead of time and put into the fridge before the main cooking.

---

1 tablespoon oil

8 noisettes of lamb

100g/4oz mushrooms, sliced

1 tablespoon plain flour

4 tablespoons jelly of your choice

2 tablespoons Worcestershire sauce

Juice of 1 lemon

150–300ml ¼–½pt stock

Salt and freshly ground black pepper

---

1. Preheat the oven to180°C/350°F/gas 4.

2. Heat the oil in a frying pan and brown the noisettes on each side. Lift out of the pan and transfer to a casserole dish.

3. Add the sliced mushrooms to the pan and fry for a few minutes, then transfer to the casserole.

4. Sprinkle the flour into the remaining oil and cook, stirring continuously, until golden.

5. Stir in the jelly, Worcestershire sauce and lemon juice. Then add sufficient stock to make a thick, smooth gravy. Season well with salt and pepper, then strain over the lamb.

6. Cover and cook in the oven for 1½ hours until tender.

Elizabethan Quince Cream

This is a beautiful, pale pink, creamy cold dessert using quince jelly for that unique quince fragrance.

450g/1lb quince or pears
50g/2oz granulated sugar
50g/2oz unsalted butter
1 heaped tablespoon of quince jelly (page 104)
½ teaspoon ground mace or cinnamon
2 tablespoons water
3 egg yolks
300ml/½pt double cream, whipped

---

1. Wash, quarter and core the fruit. Remember they are very hard so you will need a sharp knife.

2. Put the fruit into a large saucepan with the sugar, butter, jelly, spice and water. Stir for a moment to mix and then put the lid on the saucepan and simmer gently to a soft pulp, about 20 minutes.

3. Press through a sieve or blender.

4. Beat in the egg yolks whilst still hot, then leave to cool.

5. Add half of the whipped cream, incorporating it well.

6. Pour into glasses or small, pretty individual bowls and chill.

7. Decorate with the extra cream before serving.

Syllabub

This simple recipe has been prepared in kitchens for hundreds of years. Charles II of England had cows in St James's Park in London and often demanded that syllabubs were made for his table straight from the cow! This can be made a day ahead, and you can serve fruits or whichever fruit jellies you prefer under the syllabub or even mixed with it, but be careful not to take away the subtle flavour of dairy.

150ml/¼pt sweet white wine or white Martini
300ml/½pt fresh double cream
2 tablespoons brandy
Grated rind and juice of 2 lemons
Macaroon biscuits (optional)
Brandied grape jelly (page 154), spiced cranberry jelly (page 155) or of your choice

1. Put the wine or Martini, cream brandy and lemon rind and juice into a large mixing bowl and whisk until thick, when the blades of the whisk leave a trail of the mixture behind.

2. Put some macaroon biscuits, if using, into a large serving bowl or individual wine glasses, reserving a couple for decoration. Top with spoonfuls of jelly, then spoon the syllabub on top and decorate with crumbled macaroon biscuits, if using.

3. Keep in the fridge before serving.

Rose Pelargonium Sandwich Cake

An unusual but very simple and fragrant sponge cake using rose pelargonium jelly.

2-3 pelargonium leaves
100g/4oz butter
100g/4oz caster sugar
100g/4oz self-raising flour
2 large eggs
A little milk
Rose pelargonium jelly (page 66)
Icing sugar

---

1. Preheat the oven to 160°C/325°F/gas 3. Grease two 18cm/7in sandwich tins and line with baking paper.

2. Put a pelargonium leaf (or two for stronger flavour) at the bottom of each sandwich tin.

3. Cream together the butter and sugar until light and fluffy.

4. Add 1 egg at a time, beating continuously.

5. Fold in the flour. Gradually stir in 1–2 tablespoons of milk so you have a light mixture that drops off the spoon.

6. Divide the mixture equally between the tins.

7. Bake in the centre of the for 25–30 minutes until the centre is springy when lightly touched.

8. Remove from oven and transfer to a wire rack to cool slightly.

9. While still warm, spread rose pelargonium jelly generously and evenly over one sandwich cake. Place the other sandwich on top and leave to cool completely.

10. Lightly dust with icing sugar to serve. You will find that the perfume of the leaf has infused into the cake mixture.

Jellied Strawberries

This is an early twentieth-century recipe which is simple to follow and very rich in strawberry fruit flavour because it keeps the fruits whole.

1.8kg/4lb strawberries
1.4kg/3lb granulated sugar
Lemon juice

---

1. Put the strawberries and sugar into a large bowl in alternate layers and leave for 24 hours.

2. Bring very gently to the boil in the preserving pan and boil gently until the juice begins to run like syrup. Stir well.

3. When the liquid is quite sticky, add ½ teaspoon of lemon juice.

4. Put into warmed pots and tie down.

5. Label when cold.

Fruit Tartlets

These little gems can be filled with any fruit in season and then glazed with any jelly of your choice which blends in with the colour and flavour of the fruit. You can also make one large tart or little boat-shaped ones for a delicious mouthful. The tarts can be made days in advance and can be filled just before you need them as they are quite short and crumbly but irresistible.

For rich short crust pastry
150g/5oz plain flour
1 teaspoon caster sugar
Pinch of salt
75g/3oz butter
1 egg yolk
1-2 tablespoons cold water
Jelly for glaze of your choice
Fresh fruit for filling

Glazing pastry cases.

1. Preheat the oven to 180°C/350°F/gas 4 and grease some individual tartlets tins.

2. Sift the flour, sugar and salt into a bowl and rub in the butter.

3. Add the egg yolk and enough water to squeeze together the mixture to a soft dough. Chill for 15 minutes.

4. Roll out the pastry and line small tartlet tins. Prick the bases to prevent the pastry from rising.

5. Bake in the oven for 10–15 minutes, then leave to cool.

6. Put about 4 tablespoons of jelly into a small pan and melt gently. Do not allow the jelly to boil.

7. Using a glazing brush, coat the insides of the cases with the jelly. This seals the pastry from the fruit.

8. Fill the tarts with fruit – strawberries, raspberries, currants, etc. Brush the fruit very thickly with the glaze so that every part is covered. This actually holds the fruit in the case and must look glossy.

9. Serve as soon as possible with cream or just as they are.

TIP: You can also make a large tart in exactly the same way.

Glazing fruit tartlets.

Gooseberry Tansy

This is a seventeenth-century recipe. A tansy is a custard flavoured with whatever fruits are around. My mother used to make it flavoured and coloured with English marigolds. The completed dish should be the consistency of a solid omelette.

1. Cook a quart 1.2½pt) of gooseberries with some butter in a covered jar (saucepan) until quite soft.

2. Beat 4 eggs and fill them with a double handful of fine white breadcrumbs and a cupful of sugar.

3. Blend and stir this into the gooseberry pulp over a slow heat, stirring gently till the mass is cooked firm.

TIP: On no account let it get too hot or the custard will curdle.

---

1. Turn out on to a dish.

2. Sprinkle with crushed sugar and serve with hot cider or melted apple or cider jelly.

TIP: To make a successful tansy the 'nicety' of skill is to use just as much breadcrumb and egg as will take up the buttery liquid from the cooked fruit and make the same 'bind'. It may be found necessary to add another piece of butter if the fruit is very dry or more crumbs if it is too soft.

Poached Pears

A very quick and easy dessert full of autumn flavours, this uses pear and vodka jelly or pear and sloe gin. The pears can be cooked ahead of time and warmed before adding the jelly. You could serve it with two or three nasturtium flowers or blue borage flowers and cream or crème fraîche for decoration.

4 pears

Grated rind of 1 lemon

6–7 cloves

Sugar

Pot of pear and vodka jelly (page 124) or pear and sloe gin (page 144)

1. Preheat the oven to 180°C/350°F/gas 4.

2. Peel the pears, leaving the stalks in place.

3. Put into a dish with a little water and add the lemon rind and cloves. Cover with butter paper or greaseproof.

4. Poach in the oven until tender, about 15 minutes. Alternatively, you can poach the whole pears in a covered saucepan on the hob.

5. Melt the contents of jelly pot on a gentle heat in a saucepan, stirring until dissolved.

6. Pour the jelly over the cooked pears and serve with cream.

Quince Marmalet

This is an early eighteenth-century recipe from Worcester, so I've added my modern comments! Notice the difference in technique from modern recipes. In early recipes, as much goodness as possible was extracted from the fruit, hence the use of peelings.

---

4 quinces
450g/1lb loaf sugar
600ml/1pt water
A little brandy and some thin paper (see the History of Jelly)

---

1. Wipe the quinces, cut them into quarters, core them and put them into cold water to keep their colour.

2. Put the peelings and cores into cold water and boil them until tender.
This will take about 20 minutes.

3. Strain off the liquid.

4. When the liquid is cold, add the peeled quinces, weighing 450g/1lb of the fruit and 450g/1lb of loaf sugar to 600ml/1pt of liquid.

5. Boil all together until the fruit is tender, keeping them closely covered.
Remember to stir the sugar on the simmering heat until you are totally sure that the sugar has melted before boiling, otherwise you will get burnt sugar. This will take about 20 minutes. Put some jars in a warm oven to sterilise at the same time.

6. 'Beat them till they be of a right thickness.' *That would be a marmalade thickness.*

7. Pour into pre-warmed jars and, when cold, cover with brandied paper.

TIP: Alcohol acts as a steriliser and was the original way of covering the pots.

Butters and Cheeses

These are some of the first preserves made from a high proportion of fruit. The fruit is pulped, mixed with sugar or honey, then boiled down to make a thick paste. Butters are slightly less thick than the cheeses. They can both be put into oiled moulds, covered securely and kept for several years. One recipe I found particularly advised you to store the cheese for at least seven years. One hopes it hasn't been forgotten!

I have included these recipes as they link rather well with jelly making. The fruit has to be prepared a little more by removing the stalks and cores – but then after the juice has been extracted, the pulp is put through a sieve to make a smoother finish, so you are using all the fruit and there is hardly any wastage.

Damson Cheese

This recipe has come from a very old book which had lost a lot of details in the front so there is no date. I would think about the early 1800s. The one thing I can tell you is that the average cost was 8 old pence per pound! Needless to say, I added the weight conversions! These recipes would be suitable for most soft fruit and quince. Sliced up or unmoulded and served with cold meats or even cheese, they make a welcome change and, of course, there is no wastage. Notice the long, slow cooking and how they put the fruit in a 'jar'; saucepans came later.

Damsons, sugar and water

---

1. Remove the stalks and put the fruit into a large jar (*now a saucepan*) or stew pot.

2. Place in a boiling pot of cold water and cook until perfectly soft.

3. Remove the stones and pour off some of the juice which should afterwards be converted into damson jelly.

4. Add 200g/7oz sugar to each 450g/1lb fruit.

5. Continue the slow cooking for another 2 hours, then turn the whole into a preserving pan and boil rapidly for about ½ hour, stirring continuously.

6. Pour into small pots, cover closely and store in a dry, cool place.

'The housekeeper will do well to remember that mould is a plant sowing itself by multitudes of seeds, so small that they penetrate the tiniest of cracks. It spreads therefore readily from one thing to another and may sometimes lurk unsuspected on the shelves of a cupboard that is not well cleaned and aired'.
From a nineteenth-century housekeeping book.

Apple Butter

This is an old Somersetshire recipe. Cinnamon and cloves can be added with the sugar instead of lemon. If the butter is carefully made this will maintain the freshness for a couple of years or more! Apples, any kind (windfalls will do, crabs and especially Siberian crabs are, if anything, superior to orchard apples)

350g/12oz granulated sugar
to every 600ml/1pt of sieved apple pulp
Lemon juice with the grated peel to flavour

---

1. Wash and dry the fruit quickly. Quarter but do not pare the apples. Put into a preserving pan, cover with water and stew to a pulp.

2. Press through a hair.
This is a close-gauge sieve.

3. Throw away what won't go through and measure the pulp. Weigh out 350g/12oz of sugar for every 600ml/1pt of apple. Return it to the pan and boil for about an hour till quite thick.

4. Add the sugar and lemon juice and grated peel.

5. Put into pre-washed jars and, when cold, cover with paraffin wax or with a piece of brandied paper.

TIP: Use about ½ lemon to each 1.2l/2pt of pulp, but this is a matter of taste. When the sugar is dissolved, boil it up again quickly for a short time till stiff enough to spread without it running. *Remember to warm your jars.*

TIP: As an alternative, use half cider and half water when stewing the fruit.

Sloe Gin, Vodka or Brandy

There are no hard and fast rules for making sloe gin, but this is how my husband makes it.

Sloes

Sugar

Almonds or almond essence

Gin, vodka or brandy (the cheapest that you can find)

---

1. Either prick the sloes with a fork – a labour of love – or freeze the sloes, then they break naturally on de-frosting.

2. Put the prepared sloes into a large kilner jar or one with a sealed lid.

3. Pour sugar into jar to fill it a third of the way up.

4. Add 2 tablespoons of almonds or a few drops of almond essence.

5. Fill the jar to the top with gin, vodka or brandy.

6. Seal the lid, give it a few shakes and put in a larder or cool place.

7. Every couple of weeks, shake the jar vigorously.

8. After 2–3 months, strain into sterilised bottles with a screw cap, label and date. Discard the sloes.

TIP: Sloe gin will keep for many years so make sure that you date each bottle.

Elderberry Cough Mixture

This is safe for people of any age and is full of vitamin C.

450g/1lb elderberries
450g/1lb blackberries
Juice of 1 lemon
8 cloves
450g/1lb granulated sugar or honey

---

1. Put all the berries and the squeezed lemon in a pan with the cloves and simmer gently until tender, about 15 minutes.

2. Put some bottles and tops in a warm oven to sterilise.

3. Mash berries with a potato masher, then pour through muslin and leave to drip into a bowl for 2–3 hours.

4. Add the sugar and stir over a low heat until it has melted.

5. When it has completely melted, bring to the boil and boil rapidly for 2 minutes but no more, as you don't want jelly.

6. Pour immediately into the warmed bottles and cover securely.

7. Leave to cool before labelling. Keep in a cool place until needed.

TIP: The first time I made this I was so pleased until I tried to pour the mixture out. It was firmly jelly! If this happens to you melt it again in the oven to use.

Iceland Moss Jelly

Warning: This is a recipe from the nineteenth century. I don't think Iceland moss can be purchased anymore, even from a chemist – I have tried. I would not advise trying this recipe without consultation from a medical practitioner! I have included it for interest only, although certain seaweeds do have gelatinous content and could have been used.

---

4 ounces Iceland moss

1 quart /40 fl.oz water

2 ounces loaf/lump sugar

1 glass of white wine

---

1. Put the Iceland moss to boil in the water, stirring all the time it is on the fire; when it has boiled for about 45 minutes, add the loaf sugar and a glass of white wine; strain the jelly through a piece of muslin into a basin and when it is set firm and cold let it be given to the patient.

2. This jelly is most beneficial in cases of severe colds, catarrhs and all pulmonary diseases of the lungs and chest.

About the Author

Caroline Pakenham's early years were spent in the fashion industry with Christian Dior in London and eventually running her own couturier business in Exeter.

She started collecting wild produce and cooking when she sold her business in Exeter and moved to an old country manor house in a tiny hamlet on the Somerset/Wiltshire border.

She set up a small business called GREEN MAN to grow and sell fresh herbs and jellies. In addition she now gives talks and demonstrations on growing and cooking with herbs.

Caroline is married with three grown-up children.

Caroline Pakenham

Index